Simpleton Solutions

STRATEGIC EATING

THE ECONOVORE'S ESSENTIAL GUIDE

ELISE COOKE

Outskirts Press, Inc.
Denver, Colorado

Strategic Eating
The Econovore's Essential Guide
All Rights Reserved.
Copyright © 2009 Elise Cooke
V3.0

Cover Photo © 2009 JupiterImages Corporation. All rights reserved - used with permission.

Outskirts Press, Inc.
http://www.outskirtspress.com

ISBN: 978-1-4327-3212-7

Library of Congress Control Number: 2008938803

Outskirts Press and the "OP" logo are trademarks belonging to Outskirts Press, Inc.

PRINTED IN THE UNITED STATES OF AMERICA

Colossians 3:23

Thanks to my husband,
an unwitting guinea pig of many
food experiments.
Honest, Honey, I do love you!

Thanks, too, to my proofreaders,
Kathy and Julie.
You gals are awesome!

Table of Contents

Introduction
Why Write About Food Economy?

Econovore (e con' o vôr) n.
A person whose good nutrition cost him little
time, money and effort.

Food prices are rising dramatically. The subject of how to save money in this area of the budget is getting the attention it has long deserved. I say this because though food was, and still is, relatively cheap compared to ever-rising housing and energy costs, most of us were, and are, spending way more money here than we need to, usually to the detriment of nutrition as well.

Spending too much in some areas is not such a big deal. That toaster you bought before finding the identical model for a third cheaper isn't going to break you because you can amortize that loss over the ten or so years before you have to buy another one. The bread you put in it, however, you're buying at least once a week, and once it's consumed, you'll immediately have to buy it all over again. Even though each incidence is only a minor sum, the sheer repetition of overspending adds up to big bucks.

The repetition comes, of course, because you've got to eat, right? If you put away the typical three squares a day, it averages out to ninety meals a month. If each meal costs $10, that's close to a grand, but if it's only $1, it's a Benjamin, and the other nine of his brothers stay in your pocket. Food is just one area of potential savings in the family budget, but it's a big one. Is a savings of several hundred dollars a month enough to make you want to flip through a book that purports to teach sound techniques for stretching your food dollar? I'm betting that it is.

So, without further ado, here's the first technique for saving enormous amounts of money on food: Don't go to restaurants! And don't give me that "duh" eye roll, either. If your credit card issuer compiles a yearly report of your spending categories, take a quick glance at the "Dining Out" section. Ouch. Here is graphic proof that as soon as you're hungry enough, money considerations go right out the window. Esau[1] isn't the only example of how to give away your future for a bowl of stew. In restaurants, you're not only paying for the food, but also the labor, the air conditioning, the rent on the building, the guy to do the dishes, and whatever profit the proprietor can extract, so even the "family" eateries cost ten times as much as the sandwich you could have made at home. If you need to cut back on your expenses, this one's a no-brainer.

The whole book sums up this way: You save money on food by buying, well, food. By "food," I mean food all by itself; not food plus ambience, not food plus processing, not food with the nutrition sucked out of it, just food. Then you prepare the food yourself, and you don't waste it. This isn't exactly a revelation, it just requires a little discipline, planning and deliberation.

As for me, I'm not perfect, and certainly not any smarter than the average person. I learned these tips and techniques out of sheer necessity at first, and now hold to them (most of the time) as a lucrative hobby today. This book is the result of over a decade of solid research on the subject of lowering my personal food bill. I'm confident that these techniques work well, and I'm happy to share what I've learned so far. Thanks for reading!

---

[1] This is from Genesis in the Bible. Esau was born minutes ahead of his twin brother, Jacob, and therefore had the double-portion inheritance rights. However, he came in from the fields very hungry one day and gave away his first-born privilege for a bowl of red lentils. Jacob must've been a great cook.

Part I
The Art of Acquisition

Supermarkets hire whole phalanxes of professionals who do nothing more than study and implement ways to manipulate you into spending more for their products. They put the basic baking ingredients with the low profit margins at shin-level and the highly processed, high-priced foods (if you can still call them that!) right at eye-level. Packages are sized to make you buy a lot of air if you don't read the labels carefully. All those spiffy colors and cartoon characters tempt you into giving in to the children's demands. Those "basics" that you might just want to nip in for: a gallon of milk, a dozen eggs, etc.; you'll find those at the very back of the store, so that you have to run the gauntlet of eye-catching teasers reaching for your wallet. To resist these traps so carefully and cleverly set to capture your hard-earned dollars, you've got to keep your wits about you!

The next ten chapters detail some techniques for feeding your family as inexpensively as possible, without sacrificing nutrition. Most of them require no more time than what you're spending already. A couple of them may require you to learn simple new skills. Individually, each strategy  works; combined, the difference in what you spend for food will drop dramatically.

Chapter 1
When the Going Gets Tough...

Outrage can inspire. My inspiration came when I opened up the newspaper and read about the posturing of Barbara Lee. She's a congresswoman, and in June of 2007, she took it upon herself to try to eat for a week on $21, which is about what the average food stamp recipient received at the time. Her toil and tribulation enjoyed much play in the mass media and there was heard loud lamenting and wringing of hands at how tough the poor really have it trying to attain "food security" on the pittance afforded them from America's taxpayers.

I followed the story as it played out. By the end of the week, I didn't know whether to laugh or cry. Congresswoman Lee has no idea how to eat, probably for any amount of money, but certainly not on a budget! Since she held herself up as an example, so will I, and I'll demonstrate how $21 is perfectly adequate for a nutritious diet. Lee reported that she went shopping on Day One and bought:

- 2 cans of beans
- 1 can of peas
- 1 box of crackers
- 1 bag of brown rice
- 1 package of chicken thighs

- 1 package of tortillas
- 1 loaf of wheat bread
- 1 box of grits
- 2 bananas   Total: $13:37

Her first problem was readily apparent even before she even laid a hand on the shopping cart. She'd marched into the store positively broadcasting a defeatist attitude, to wit: "We want to raise awareness of the difficulties faced by low income people in obtaining a healthy diet." Since she'd pretty much predetermined that a healthy diet wasn't feasible with these funds, my guess is that's why she didn't even attempt to buy much nutritious food. Look at the outsized carbohydrate load in her cart: peas, crackers, rice, tortillas, bread, grits and bananas. Then there's the appalling quantity of convenience food, which lowers nutrition and/or raises price: canned foods, prepared tortillas, crackers and bread.

I could go on, but let me instead offer my list, if I were on this budget:

- 1 lb pinto beans - $1.09
- 2 lbs brown rice - $1.70
- 5 lbs white flour - $3.19
- 5 lbs whole wheat flour - $3.99
- 1 package yeast - $.72
- 18 oz peanut butter - $1.99
- 1 4-lb whole chicken - $4.00
- 1 bunch celery $1.49
- 1.5 lbs carrots - $1.50   Total: $19.67[2]

Okay, so this first week might seem a bit dull, lacking much in the way of variety, but a human body can thrive on this. (I'm also not going to shoplift condiments from fast food restaurants!) The beans and rice combine to make a complete protein and filling meals. One package of yeast and the flours yield plenty of sourdough bread, tortillas and crackers. Nothing will go to waste: bones, giblets, celery

---

[2] All prices were found on Safeway.com 6/3/08, except for the chicken. I regularly find it on sale there for $.69/lb, but on this date it was $1.69, so I "compromised" a bit, since it's $.90/lb at Costco. It should also be noted that food prices had a record inflation run between mid-2007 and mid-2008.

leaves and carrot peels make soup stock and rendered fat will grease the skillet. Cooked and raw vegetables provide essential vitamins. Peanut butter on whole wheat is the new breakfast of champions, and another complete protein. At the end of the week, I'll at least have some flour, yeast and peanut butter left over, giving me effectively more money to spend next week. So, I'll replenish what I need and probably splurge on an onion. In subsequent

You can read about the Congressional Food Stamp Challenge for yourself at: http://foodstampchallenge.typepad.com

weeks, I'll keep accumulating extra money until I can work up to afford some savings strategies that require a little capital outlay, such as growing vegetables from seed and bulk-buying groceries, and I'll have even more cash for cheese, eggs, oil, and so on. In short, my list considers sustainability.

Our congresswoman reported that after her shopping trip she decided to skip breakfast and go to McDonald's for lunch, where she blew another $1.10 for a McChicken sandwich. On Day Three, she hits Taco Bell for a $.79 taco. Day Five, she goes to White Castle and gets a burger for $1.02. I don't need to tell you she finished out the week hungry, broke and complaining that "people forced to eat on such a budget could develop health problems." Certainly, I'm getting heart palpitations just thinking of the choices she makes with taxpayers' money!

Okay, so Barbara Lee is just one person with her poor planning. I could have dismissed her as an aberration. Then I kept reading. It turns out several other California congresspersons took the challenge, and from what I could see, they all came to the same conclusions that Lee did. The common "wisdom" from the political sphere and the media is that the poor are suffering much higher rates of obesity than the general population in part because "fatty food is cheap;" therefore, "low family income may be the single most powerful contributing factor in childhood obesity."[3]

My family of five regularly eats for about $8 a day, and we could definitely do better, so when Barbara Lee's words were splashed all over the newspapers, I expected to soon be reading rebuttals from the

---

[3] Time Magazine, June 23, 2008, "It's Not Just Genetics."

"experts," but I must have missed them. I then waited for letters to the Editor from savvy home economists, and waited, and waited. And waited. The real kicker was when I got a hold of the USDA's official "Cost of Food at Home" guide and discovered that our government doesn't even think a two-year old can eat for $21 a week.

Clearly we're losing some valuable skills in this country, just when the economy is circling the drain and we're going to need them. We've forgotten how to plan ahead and think strategically to maximize what our resources can provide, and so to maintain our standard of living, we're in hock up to our eyeballs, and/or demanding more from the government.

Let's go back to my list again for a minute. I wanted to show how one person can eat healthfully on what the government provides through the Food Stamp program, even assuming he/she

Check out http://www.cnpp.usda.gov/USDAFoodCost-Home.htm for a good cry.

had pay full price at only one supermarket and didn't get help anywhere else. Mission accomplished, I think. However, there is so much more I could do to stretch those dollars even further. For instance, who's to say you have to go this alone? Why not buddy up with some like-funded friends so we could buy in bulk? This way, those pinto beans and rice would only cost $.50/lb each, and we'd save at least another couple of greenbacks on the flours, yeast and carrots. Now I can afford a gallon of milk this week. Nonfat is cheaper than regular; so much for the mantra that the poor can only afford fatty food.

Pooling resources to save through bulk purchases is one helpful strategy in making food dollars stretch, but there are more. I could have chatted up the produce manager at the store to see if there are any past-their-prime onions and other veggies to be had for cheap. In soup stock, aesthetics don't matter. If I'd skipped the poultry aisle and stuck to vegetarian protein combinations, I'd likely have more variety, too. Lentils, whole grains and nuts are filling, relatively cheap and very nutritious.

If my every dollar counted so critically, why wouldn't I take advantage of some good old-fashioned capitalism? We have a good selection of grocery stores in this country, all competing for my patronage. If I comparison-shopped at a couple of different stores at least, I would undoubtedly be able to buy some of my market basket for less than the prices I quoted earlier.

Assuming I didn't spend to my last dollar every week and instead built up a surplus of funds, I could also take great advantage of some of those "once in a blue moon" sales that stores have as loss leaders or clearance items. For example, if some store practically gives away peanut butter for $.99/lb, I want to be ready to buy six-months' worth. It may look a little weird under the bed, but it'll keep, and I'll have saved a lot of money by planning ahead.

Finally, there's the savings strategy I can't stress enough. Look at all the money I didn't spend on junk. Even one Twinkie™, soda or bag of chips would have taken away a significant amount of the resources needed to buy quality food. I remember reading an article in Parade Magazine a few years ago about "Hunger in America," where a chief complaint of the profiled "hungry" families was that they couldn't take their children to McDonald's more often. Somehow, I can't rally behind higher taxes or deeper national debt to give the poor more nights out.

So, why did I just spend several pages, proving to the cusp of readership somnolence, that a person in the United States could eat well for $21 a week? What was the point, exactly? Just this: How much are you spending per week, per person? This isn't an idle question. The difference in monthly food bills between two families of equal size living side-by-side can be hundreds of dollars. Strategically thinking about how to spend your money in this area will make great strides in your overall financial security, and your health.

Chapter 2
Nutrition is Number One

There's more to this food finesse thing than saving money. Shoot, you could eat dirt and save buckets of money. The challenge is to eat nutritiously; otherwise, what's the point?

For the record, I am no nutrition expert. Like you, I try to research and understand the basics. We'll start with protein since we need it to build cells, hemoglobin in blood and a few other physiological functions that are hard to ignore. The general rule of thumb is that about ten to fifteen percent of your calories should be protein, but anything in excess of that ratio doesn't cause any harm in healthy people. In fact, most U.S. citizens consume more than their fair share of protein (usually along with too much fat) without even thinking about it.

Even though protein deficiency is really not an issue here, understanding the mechanics of this vital component in our diets is important from a meal-planning perspective. Proteins are comprised of amino acids; of the 20 or so amino acids that make up our protein, only 8 can't be manufactured in our bodies, so they are called the "essential amino acids." Generally, animal proteins like meats, eggs and dairy have all of those, but vegetable sources don't. If you're just eating plants, you have to combine what's missing from one source with another to make up the complete protein. Research strongly suggests that the complements don't have to be eaten in the same meal to get the nutritional benefit, as long as it's in the same day.

Fortunately, certain categories of plants tend to combine easily to make complete proteins. In general, legumes (beans, lentils, peas, garbanzo beans, etc.) combine with grains (brown rice, whole wheat, oats, and so forth) or seeds (flax, sesame, pumpkin...) or nuts (any kind but your in-laws) to provide all the essential amino acids. Soy is a decent protein all by itself. Combining a plant source with a small amount of an animal source also supplies what is missing.

So, in practical terms, what does a complete protein look like? Some common meals include bean and barley soup, oatmeal and milk, hummus (which has garbanzo beans coupled with sesame seeds), rice and beans, peanut butter or cheese on whole wheat, nut or seed breads, bean burrito, buckwheat pancakes with nuts, and on and on and on. You'll find these healthy combinations in old family recipes that long predate the scientific research on amino acids or Ph.D.'s in Nutrition.

Vitamins and minerals are important, too, of course, but as luck would have it, the foods that contribute to protein by and large provide many of those as well. Fresh vegetables and fruits also contribute quite a bit. Produce that is particularly vitamin and mineral dense includes kale (A, C, K calcium, manganese), spinach (B1, B2, B3, B6, folate, C, K, potassium, calcium, magnesium, iron, zinc), broccoli (B2, B6, folate, C, A, K, potassium, calcium, magnesium, iron, zinc), tomatoes (B1, B6, folate, C, A) and watermelon (B1, B6, potassium).

It's a good idea to convert all those Betty Crocker recipes, like for waffles, to use at least half whole wheat flour. Of course, all white flour would make the waffles even cheaper to produce. However, my family has to last all morning on this food, and they need good quality to do it. Whole grains, along with the eggs and milk in the recipe, are important to that goal. I can't take my eye off the nutritional ball just to save a few pennies. (Better yet, I could even add flax seeds or walnuts to the mix!) The downside, of course, is

Foods that may not be a regular feature on your shopping list, but are really healthy include: seaweed, quinoa, and calf's liver.

that the food sometimes costs more. We saw earlier how even living on food stamps a person can achieve a healthful diet by avoiding junk and only buying foods that have good nutritional "bang for the buck." I can also see how many people of limited means could get into trouble by deciding to "treat" themselves with junk food once in a while, leaving paltry resources for obtaining quality. Don't fall into this trap. Diabetes, obesity and heart disease are more costly than any funds you could save by making cost the only consideration in food purchasing.

Eggs and non-fat dairy products are also among those foods that are somewhat pricey, especially now, but they're worth buying because they are incredibly nutrient-dense. Whole grains and fresh produce should also factor somewhere into every meal. Any discussion of saving money in this book first considers the ramifications of healthful eating, then the cost.

Chapter 3
The Larder for Starters

The supermarket is a good place to people-watch. Most shoppers are there at least weekly, pulling things off the shelves based on what they plan to eat in the very near future. They may have been motivated in their menu choices by the fact that spaghetti noodles are on sale, so they buy one of those, and then pay full price for the sauce and hamburger. Then there are the partiers, buying the hotdogs, ice and alcohol. They need it today, and money is no object. Watch out for the coupon queens; they're moving and reading at the same time and may not see you as they look for all the highly processed foods they're loading into the cart.[4]

Then there's that really weird shopper. Looking at his cart, you can't figure out for the life of you how he's going to make meals out of what he's buying. Seven packages of spaghetti noodles? Fifteen pounds of pork shoulder on clearance? A case of off-brand loss-leader peanuts? Is this some bad imitation of a Thai recipe? For fifty people?

If you want to maximize your food savings, aspire to be the weird one. He's not shopping with the week's food needs in mind. His singular goal is to find the lowest prices on nutritious foods he

---

[4] When was the last time you saw a coupon for fresh produce or flour?

eats, and when he finds a good deal, he loads up as much as he can reasonably store at home, preferably a several months' supply.

He still needs to eat, so how is he putting the week's meals together? Not a problem. First, he cuts up the pork into meal-size portions, labels them, and heads to the freezer. While he's putting the pork away, he grabs a pound of hamburger from his freezer to thaw. He smiles wistfully, remembering how he bought it for $.99/lb, and how the checkout clerk looked at him when he bought 25 pounds.

Stashing the peanut butter, he looks for his spaghetti sauce. There it is, right next to his pasta bin, a store brand he bought for $.99. He also puts most of his pasta away, reserving one package of spaghetti noodles, and one jar of sauce. He'll need those for tonight, along with the hamburger, for dinner.

The price shopper doesn't look so strange when you see what he's actually eating. In fact, he and the "weekly shopper" even have a meal in common. Let's compare their spaghetti dinners, just for fun.

Both took advantage of the noodles on sale ($.69/lb), so they're at parity there. However, I mentioned Price Shopper's spaghetti sauce is only $.99 per jar. Weekly Shopper didn't do so well. She paid $2.39 for her jar. PS's hamburger was $.99; WS bought hers for $2.50. To keep this simple, let's say they both spent the same amount for side dishes and drinks, so PS only beats WS on two dinner items. Still, WS paid $2.91 more for her dinner than PS did.

So, big deal, three bucks difference. Well, there are a few factors to consider here:

1. Shopping only for low prices takes no more time, energy or effort than shopping for the weekly menu.

2. Even if the average savings for this strategy is only $2.91 all day, (and I contend that it's usually much more), over the course of a year, that's still over $1000.

3. Keeping a pantry stocked means that you can always find something to eat, even if you're too busy to get to the store.

4. A stocked pantry is also a good idea for emergencies when stores might be closed for days. The government usually

recommends that we keep a four-day supply of food available, but the reality for a big disaster could require more, or you can be in a position to help others.

5. You can insulate yourself somewhat from general food inflation by "buying low and eating high," that is, getting the food as cheaply as you can in quantities that will last you up to a year means that what you're paying the price of the day you bought it, even if even the new "bottom" sale price goes up at the store, due to inflation.[5]

6. A well-stocked pantry presents you with choices. Choices lend themselves to acceptable substitutions. Those substitutions save money by "tiding you over" until the desired food goes back on sale. In other words, you can wait out the time that chicken is at top-dollar prices even if run out of stock, because you still have the turkey you bought for $.30/lb.

7. You can also save gas and time. If you've got plenty for meals in your pantry, why go to the supermarket this week? No laws will be broken, honest.

This method shopping for the purpose of storing and preparing meals that are the lowest possible price in their entirety is often referred to as the "Pantry Principle." There's absolutely no extra work involved, just a shift in thinking. When you head to the grocery store, the focus is not on what you're going to eat that week, but what's a good deal. You then develop your meal plan based on what you've got at home. That's it. I wish every cost-cutting idea in life could be so easy.

---

[5] No joke, you can make more money this way than if you put the equivalent funds in a certificate of deposit!

Chapter 4
Sow, Sow Savings

Step outside and look around. If there's anywhere that gets at least six hours of sun somewhere where you live, it's a good bet that you can grow some of your own food. You might have been discouraged by those fussy gardening books that insist that you have to plant by the light of a full moon, perfectly calibrate soil pH for each planting, fertilize with peat, green soil and worm castings, while administering daily fish emulsion side dressings, so you came away with the feeling that this vegetable gardening thing was more time, expense and effort than it was worth. If you want vegetables to exhibit at the County Fair, feel free to handpick each individual aphid off of the leaves with tweezers, but some of us have better things to do. I estimate that my total time in the garden averages out to about an hour a week. Once you set up the basic conditions for a plant to grow, that's generally just what it wants to do, with very little effort from you, and will reward you with a decent amount of food for little more than the cost of water.

The phrase "dirt cheap" used to mean something, and really, it still can. A successful garden does not need bagfuls of expensive composts, topsoils, peat moss and fertilizers. Your yard clippings, spent plants, leaves and kitchen scraps, diligently composted, will yield the vast majority of what your vegetables need. If you can get a cheap or free source of livestock manure, that is wonderful for your soil. Plenty of websites and gardening books tell you how to check for mineral deficiencies; don't run out and buy anything until you know you need it.

Composted tree leaves don't contribute a lot of nitrogen, but they're great for soil-building and provide important trace elements that their deep roots have soaked up.

A lot of food can be had with a surprisingly small amount of space. Don't overlook the possibilities of setting up some containers on the patio or balcony! In my own case, I made about 500 square feet of little garden plots wherever the kids wouldn't trample on them, and not all have optimal sun conditions, but I'm able to grow most of our vegetables, and a lot of our fruit. Various approaches help make this possible:

Grow What You Eat. This would seem obvious, but some gardeners grow large amounts of only one or two types of vegetables, resulting in too much of a good thing, and not enough of anything else. Other gardeners read that certain plants do well in their area, so

For a good example of the potential of growing a lot of food in a very small space, go to: www.earthtainer.org. It's amazing what a little backyard tinkering can accomplish.

they grow those, but their families don't really care for the produce. What a waste!

Try to plant with real meals in mind. This will leave room for other crops. In our case, we don't bother with zucchini, Brussels sprouts, or radishes, no one's going to eat them except under torture. Instead, we devote large amounts of space to tomatoes because everyone loves them and I can make spaghetti sauce out of whatever's left.

Another planting consideration is how much produce your family can use at a time. We'll plant only about 30 bush beans at a time, which takes up about 2 square feet, staggered every three weeks or so, to get just the right number we can eat. A two-month stand of spinach for five people is also only a couple of square feet; harvest the outer leaves and let the plants make more between cuttings. I sprinkle a few onion seeds just about anywhere there's a little space; they can be harvested any time in their growth, and they repel a lot of insect pests. Ideally, when you go out to harvest for the day's meals, you'll find just enough ripe for the day. Anything more will either be wasted or require more effort to find a place for it.

Grow Up. No, not you, the plants. More than tomatoes and pole beans can take cages; try cucumbers, melons and squash. If the produce gets heavy, support with a flexible sling. Old pantyhose is a classic support material. I've heard the same about old bras!

Use the Same Space at the Same Time. This is also known as "companion planting." A typical example of plants sharing space is the combination of corn, pole beans and pumpkins. Corn grows up tall. Pole beans planted near the base can climb the corn, and low-lying pumpkin vines shade the roots, discourage weeds and keep water from evaporating out of the soil. It's a win all around. Onions, dill, oregano, sage, mint, chives, coriander, rosemary, sage and other herbs have insect-repelling properties, so they are often planted among leafy greens. Lettuces like a bit of shade, especially when the weather starts to get very warm, so plants that can overshadow them, like bush beans, carrots and cucumbers do well. Deep-rooted plants like carrots paired with shallower-rooted plants like onions, beans and peas also help each other.

Use the Same Space Serially. I admit I live in the enviable USDA Zone 9, which allows me to grow some things year round, but even if you live in a shorter season, you can maximize food output from the soil by double or triple-cropping in your garden spaces. An example of this might be growing salad greens or snap peas from early to late

> Find out what the USDA zone is for where you live at:
> http://www.usna.usda.gov/Hardzone/ushzmap.html

Spring, followed by bush beans until mid-Summer, and then pumpkins or other Winter squash until late Fall. It helps to start the next planting in pots and then transplant when ready.

Extend the Season. As long as tomatoes don't freeze, they'll keep ripening, slowly. Cover them when nighttime temperatures drop below the 50's Fahrenheit, and you can have tomatoes for

Thanksgiving. With a simple cold frame, you can have salad greens even when it's snowing outside. The added bonus to growing in cold weather is that the water needs of your plants are almost nil, so you're getting produce for the cost of seed and no more. On the other end of the year, start seeds in the warm indoors and plant outside when the weather is amenable.

Based on my notes the last couple of years, here is what my year-round harvest looks like, depending upon what I'm in the mood to grow. Note that unless stated otherwise, whatever was being harvested in the previous month, still is.

- **All Year**: Ready: carrots, onions (greens or bulbs), garlic (greens or bulbs), chard, lemons, sprouts
- **December, January and February:** Ready: broccoli, beets, cabbage, lettuce[6], oranges, parsnips, turnips[7]
- **March and April:** Ready: snap peas, basil (indoors)
- **May:** Finished: broccoli, beets, lettuce and oranges. Ready: artichokes, celery, peaches
- **June:** Finished: artichokes, cabbage, parsnips, peaches and turnips. Ready: potatoes, tomatoes, blackberries, cucumbers, green beans, basil (outdoors)
- **July:** Finished: blackberries. Ready: corn, peppers
- **August:** Ready: melons
- **September and October:** Finished: corn and green beans. Ready: pumpkins, grapes, apples, ground cherries
- **November:** Finished: tomatoes, apples, grapes, peppers, tomatoes, potatoes, ground cherries, cucumbers, basil. November and the first part of December are our leanest harvest months, as the garden gets "reset" into Winter Mode.[8]

With a garden, of course I'm getting organic produce with peak nutritional content. By the time we start to get tired of something, a new harvest is ripening. Meal planning is in some ways easier, as I

---

[6] Beet greens, chard leaves, lettuce, carrots and sprouts make for quite nice Winter salads.

[7] Don't like turnips? Try rutabagas. They're practically indistinguishable from turnips in recipes, but milder-tasting.

[8] This is when space is a challenge for me. Just when most of my Summer stuff is putting out its last "hurrah," I need to plant for Winter crops.

just work with what's available. In the Winter, what we have lends itself well to hearty soups, stews and breads. Springtime means a lot of green salads, steamed veggies and stir fries. In the Summer and Fall, we enjoy tomato/basil/cucumber salads, pasta with tomato sauces, corn, anything grilled and lots of fresh fruit.

I read an article recently where a mom was congratulating herself for getting her kids more interested in eating vegetables because she let them select what they wanted at her local farmer's market. I'm glad that works, but I can tell you that when children have invested the time and effort to plant the food, they eagerly watch it grow until it often doesn't even make it to the kitchen, which is just fine with me. Gardening provides low-cost, healthy and better-tasting food, moderate exercise and a fun activity the whole family can enjoy. Why gardening is largely considered just a hobby and not a viable savings and health-promoting practice is beyond me. In fact, during World War II, home "Victory Gardens" produced fully forty percent of the nation's produce, and helped us win the war.

I haven't emphasized the energy and carbon-savings aspect of gardening because the book is largely geared toward the economic advantages of home food production. However, the food you grow wasn't treated with petroleum-based fertilizers and wasn't shipped from continent to continent by jet and truck. This is a significant "win" whether you're motivated by patriotism or fighting global warming, or both.

Finally, food you don't consume can be used elsewhere. Some areas of the world are facing dangerous famines and shortages, and your garden can do its small part to alleviate suffering. So, grab a shovel and get to work!

A little history lesson on Victory Gardens: http://en.wikipedia.org/wiki/Victory_garden

Chapter 5
Water and Energy

T he sunshine here in California is free, and that's about it. Everything else is costly and taxed to the hilt. To save on my food bill, I have to be very careful to factor in the cost of the energy and water used to produce and prepare it. The highest rate I pay for electricity is a staggering $.31 per Kilowatt Hour, and water runs me $.004 per gallon, which is almost half a penny. (There's also talk of rationing again this year.) I'm pretty sure we pay among the highest rates for any services in the country, and likely soon after this book comes out, I'll reread this chapter and be nostalgic for these low, low prices.

Let's look at the gardening issue first. If I'm paying $1.69 for that packet of seeds[9] and as much as I do for water, am I actually coming out ahead of grocery store prices? How do I figure this out?

Luckily for me, I do know roughly how much water I'm using per plant. I installed a drip system. This cost me about $100 three years ago, plus about $5-10 in new pieces every year, but I save a ton

---

[9] That price of course is at the peak of the planting season. But go to your local grocery, drug and hardware stores around late June or early July, and you'll find that packets are practically given away. Most seeds will keep until the following year.

of water delivering the precious liquid right to the roots, so I'm pretty sure it's already paid for itself. I use drippers that allow 8 gallons per hour to leak through them, and one dripper more or less goes to one plant. I also have automatic timers that turn the water on for about 20 minutes every other day. Since 10 minutes is a sixth of an hour, I get roughly 1.33 gallons, or half a penny's worth of water to each plant each day, on average.

Plants have different days-to-harvest times, usually conveniently printed on the seed packet. Just for the sake of this exercise, let's assume that on average a plant lasts for 90 days before its useful life is over. Let's also assume there are about 40 viable seeds on average in each seed packet. So, each plant will receive roughly $.45 worth of water, and costs about $.04 to purchase[10] and therefore needs to produce more than $.49 worth of food for it to be economically worthwhile.

If I'm comparing what I grow to the cheapest way I can buy it at the grocery store, pesticides and all, carrots from the garden cost roughly half of that. Tomatoes are a huge win; what costs a dollar at the store is only a few pennies at home. Just about everything else comes out somewhere in between. Obviously, buying organic, which is a fairer comparison, yields even better savings. But the point is, even at my ridiculous water rates, and even competing with producers who don't have to pay nearly as much for water as I do, I save money by growing as much as I can at home.

Gas and electricity factor mostly into food preparation. Since local restaurants have to pay the same painful energy prices I do, I can be confident I come out ahead by not eating out. My real competition is with "convenience" food. If those Frosted Flakes were made somewhere with cheap labor and other cheap overhead, I could then save money if I slept in every morning and just let the kids pour their own bowls. To research whether or not I'm better off monetarily by using more energy with home-prepared foods, I first went to my energy utility's website, which had a link to analyze energy usage for common appliances. Ovens apparently run around 2300 watts/hour, stove tops 1000 watts/hour, microwave ovens 1500 watts/hour, slow cookers 200 watts/hour and dishwashers 2800 watts/hour. For small meals, it pays to use a toaster oven, which

---

[10] In addition to post-season seeds, this can be offset somewhat from seeds saved from the produce of the previous year.

clocks in at a slim 1200 watts/hour. If I run my oven for an hour a day and wash dishes once, it adds at most $1.50 to the day (at the highest rate), or $.50/meal on average; individual meal mileage may vary. Slow cooking is a good deal; 10 hours in a CrockPot is cheaper than one in the oven. I often use a pressure cooker, which cuts stovetop time to about a third. The sad epilogue to all this analysis is that staying in bed is still not a money-saving option. I'll write to my congressperson.

Hmmm, is an hour a reasonable average oven time per day, i.e. per every three meals? This number can go way down with a few tweaks to meal preparation. First, don't cook one meal, cook several at once. Cram the oven as full as possible every time it's on. Bread bakes at close to the same temperature for a roast, or cookies. Pizza and pumpkin pie

> Go to
> http://www.energyguide.com
> to do your own energy-usage
> sleuthing.

can share space. Dry bread crumbs or make croutons with the latent heat from a falling oven. Make large batches of the same thing for several meals' worth. Some families swap cooking nights with other families; they make enough for both on their days, in exchange for a night off when it's their friends' turn.

I haven't mentioned much about natural gas because even with my dryer, water heater and stovetop all on gas, I pay the lowest rate at $1.45/therm. A therm, by the way, is 100,000 British thermal units (BTU), which is the equivalent of burning 100 cubic feet of natural gas at "standard temperature and pressure," (STP). I don't personally use a lot of them compared to the electric portion of the bill, so I haven't researched cost savings in this area as extensively. However, the same principles of energy savings in food preparation also apply to saving therms versus kilowatts; the more at once, the better the savings.

"Once a Month Cooking," by Mimi Wilson and Mary Beth Lagerborg, takes advantage of the economies of scale in shopping, effort and energy use by developing a plan for a month's worth of dinners, then doing all the preparation and cooking in one marathon session, usually a weekend. The resultant meals are frozen, thawed and reheated later, but even running the microwave for a few minutes every night, you'd come out ahead on energy costs. I'm intrigued by the concept, even if it won't work for me because my garden won't generally put out that much produce at once, and I wouldn't be as flexible to use up leftovers or take advantage of the lowest price of every ingredient in the meals. Still, if you're really crunched for time during the weekdays, you'll get significant savings in both money and time using this strategy versus resorting to convenience foods, so it's worth a mention.

To save energy, it helps to think outside the oven. The Internet is a Wonderland of interesting ideas in this regard and people willing to share them. Run a search engine for "solar cooker" and let the World Wide Web regale you with every design imaginable to harness the sun for cooking food. This is a win on two fronts: You cook the food for free and don't add heat to the house on a hot day. Another interesting, and old-fashioned concept that predates the modern slow cooker is to bring food to boiling on the stove, then turn off the heat and insulate it very well. The trapped heat can cook the food for hours longer. A variation of the theme is to dig a small pit in the backyard, place hot coals in the bottom and then put a heavy Dutch oven over it. The smoldering coals work like a slow cooker.

In any case, if I can get that energy total for a day's worth of meals down to the equivalent of 20 minutes of oven time, then the added cost is less than $.20/meal. The higher number still saved money, but that $.30/day differential is over $100 at the end of the year. Those of you with well water and solar cells on the roof can laugh all the way to the bank, but the even the rest of us will still come out ahead growing and cooking our own food.

Chapter 6
Time and Space

Oh, no! Is astrophysics a requirement for understanding the economics of the family food budget? Thankfully, no. For one thing, time is relative in space. Here on Planet Earth, time won't slow down for anything. And it's finite. As for space, the universe may be still expanding, but my cupboards aren't getting the hint. I've touched on the precepts of "time and space economy" in other chapters, but it would be a good idea to concentrate on strategies to increase efficiency.

There is something more rare and therefore precious than money, and that is time. The whole point of saving money is to save time; that is, the time that would be otherwise spent to earn the money that was wasted. The concept of frugality thus refers to time and personal involvement, not just money. Here are some ideas on how to work "smarter, not harder," as far as food is concerned.

Minimize movement for common tasks. No one wants to bake a lot when the flour is in one cupboard clear across the kitchen from the sugar. It took me a while to work this out for myself. Making muffins or a simple cake used to mean opening, retrieving and putting back ingredients in at least 4 different places, all of them a long hike from my workspace. Finally, it dawned on me to clean out the cupboard directly over the stand mixer (duh!) and fill it with as many baking ingredients as possible. I commandeered the drawer right under that counter for measuring spoons, cups, spatulas, and so forth, and the cupboard below that holds muffin tins, pie plates, mixing bowls and liquid measure cups. I can now make bread, cakes, pies, tortillas, tempura mix, granola, crepes, cookies, brownies, muffins, waffles, biscuits, cobbler toppings, you name it, faster than it takes the oven to preheat.

Pay attention to how you work in the kitchen as you prepare meals, and how much travel is involved to accomplish ordinary tasks. Maybe the savory spices should inhabit the cupboard between the stove top and oven. After noticing that I walked back and forth across the kitchen at least twice a day to make tea, I finally moved my hot water maker to where I was storing the tea bags and mugs. The pantry keeps current with a little of everything I use commonly; I refill containers when needed from longer-term storage elsewhere. Flatware is in the drawer closest to the kitchen table. Dishes are right over the dishwasher. In short, my kitchen is arranged as efficiently as I can get it for the way I do things, and I'm constantly looking at ways to improve it, much to the consternation of the other household members who can't count on anything being anywhere anymore. I can't stress enough how much efficient storage saves in both directions, pulling out and putting back.

Consider getting a few good tools. A stand mixer is a wonderful thing. While it's whipping cream, cutting butter into flour for that flaky pie crust, or kneading bread, you can be emptying the dishwasher and scrubbing the kitchen table. The good kind of pass-this-on-to-your-grandkids-quality mixers run a few hundred bucks, so hint broadly around Christmas-time for some relatives to pool together. You don't need most of the attachments. Just the basic mixing paddle, whisk and dough hook are plenty to make the vast majority of common meals.

Pressure cookers came up earlier, in the energy savings chapter. Ordinarily, water can't go much higher than 212 degrees Fahrenheit (100C) before boiling away, but when water vapor is trapped and pushes up the pressure to 10 lbs per square inch, the temperature increases to 250 degrees (121C). This allows food to cook much faster, without losing water, so it gets very tender, too. Cheap cuts of meat are falling off the bone after only 45 minutes at pressure. Beans and rice take about half an hour. Artichokes only need about seven or eight minutes before they're practically falling apart. Apples to soften for sauce barely even need to come to pressure. When the weight on the top starts rocking, turn down the heat a bit so the temperature doesn't keep rising, and start the timer.

Slow cookers, like the CrockPot™, also got an Honorable Mention in the energy savings contest. They themselves may take a long time, but you don't have to be involved, so it's a timesaver for you. For a main course, you can usually assemble the meal in the morning, turn the cooker on, and serve in the evening. This is great for making stock, soup, chili, meats,

> Check out your local thrift shops for small kitchen appliances, especially slow cookers. My guess is that people get rid of them when they're moving because they're bulky. There's the risk of buying something that's broken, but they don't really have any moving parts, so it's hard to break one of these things. I got mine at St. Vincent de Paul for $5 years ago, and it still works great.

stews... Run an Internet search on "slow cooker recipes" for inspiration.

There are still a few holdouts in the U.S. who don't own a microwave oven. These can be had for under a hundred bucks, and are good for reheating something, softening butter, steaming vegetables quickly, etc. Besides saving time, they save energy because the microwave oven doesn't need to run for very long compared to a conventional oven.

Store only ingredients and nutritious foods. Flour, baking powder and soda, sugar and chocolate take up much less space than bread mix, brownie mix, pancake mix, etc. Bottled and canned drinks also take up a lot of space, cost orders of magnitude more than tap water, and provide little nutritional value.[11]

Clear off the kitchen counter! You need room to work, especially if you're making several meals at once. Create, and jealously guard, one long flat area and keep your tools and ingredients within easy reach.

---

[11] But if ads are to be believed, soft drinks make you more athletic, good-looking and popular, so there's that.

....But keep out what you use. This would seem to be the opposite of the previous point, but efficiency is lost if you're getting out and putting things back over and over again. My stand mixer probably figures somewhere into two meals out of every three, so the most work I'm doing to retrieve it or put it away is to slide it back and forth out of a corner of my "working counter." However, the standing electric slicer is tucked deep into a cupboard and only sees the light of day once every six months or so. I keep jelly roll pans and cutting boards propped up against the wall on the counter; I'll put them away for company, but they get used enough to justify their place. (Many cooks hang things on the walls and overhead; I would love to, but would likely lose an eye on a frying pan handle.)

Make some room. When non-perishables go on some terrific sale, buy a year's supply if you can. To store it, you may have to part with the pants you haven't worn since high school, sorry. It goes without saying that you'll need some kind of storage system so you can keep track of what you have.

Keep the kitchen clean. One fateful day, our family returned home after a week away, opened the door, and started to gag. A horrible stench permeated everything. Fearful that some large animal (or, gulp, person?) had died in the place while we were gone, my husband and I left the kids on the front porch and cautiously stepped inside.

We found our problem in the kitchen. I'd cut up some chicken carcasses for the trip, and tossed the extra skin and bones in the trash....which I'd forgotten to take to the dumpster outside. That was bad enough, but the truly horrifying part was that maggots had thrived in the nice warm house with the rotting meat. There was a conga line of the creatures stretching across the kitchen. Flies were piled up in black drifts at every windowsill. Ants had invaded, too, and they were helping themselves to the maggots. This was like something straight out of "The Amityville Horror."

After a week of camping in the woods, this was just too much. We went out to eat. For two straight days. It took that much deep cleaning before the house felt sanitary enough to eat in again.

Hopefully your messes aren't so extreme, but when the kitchen's a wreck, so are your meal plans. Don't wake up to a sink full of dirty dishes; you'll be behind the Eight Ball all day. Clean during those spaces in time during meal preparation while you're waiting for onions or hamburger to brown, something to heat up in the microwave or something to mix. And, whatever you do, "always take the garbage out!"[12]

Think ahead. Plan meals in advance, preferably by a few days. Don't get settled on the menu too far ahead or you won't have the flexibility to take advantage of a good sale of something perishable, or use up leftovers from the fridge. After dinner each night, figure out what's to be served for the next day so you can soak the beans, thaw the pot roast overnight, or even do some prep work, especially if there isn't going to be time tomorrow. Consider what's going to be needed for the week. It's just as easy to make enough rice to go with the stir fry today as it is to double that amount for lunches later. This is the concept of "planned leftovers;" cooking extra of one or more ingredients as part of one meal to use in the future. Make several meals' worth of whatever you're making, then on a busy day, dinner is just a microwave away. Being deliberate in meal-planning, especially the night before, can keep the overall average preparation time for dinners down to 20 minutes or less. Even two full-time wage-earners can manage nutritious, low-cost meals in that period of time.

Use your freezer effectively. When planning meals, scan for what needs to be used up, first from the refrigerator, then the garden, then the freezer. Meats need to be used within about six months, so keep a steady rotation going in the freezer, and at least some kind of system so you know what's there, and how old it is. Label carefully! I've learned from frustrating experience that whatever looks obvious in the clear plastic bag at room temperature is impossible to discern once frosted over. If you can freeze something flat in a gallon-size freezer bag, it'll stack like a book against the walls and save space.

What should be in your freezer? Ideally, most of the space should be devoted to complete entrees ready to reheat, and sale meat. A batch of muffins or cookies for surprise guests or other obligations never hurts, if you can spare the room. Try to avoid storing a lot of fruits and vegetables. Consume them fresh, or can them.[13]

Now is as good a time as any to suggest buying an extra freezer to take advantage of good meat (and other) sales. Meat prices

---

[12] "Sarah Cynthia Sylvia Stout Would Not Take the Garbage Out," Shel Silverstein, 1974. It's a very funny poem.
[13] There's more on canning in Chapter Nine.

especially are wildly divergent over the course of a year, it's not that hard to save enough money to gain back the cost of the freezer and the extra electricity to run it within just a couple of years. This is especially true if you have a large family.

In general, chest freezers which open at the top use less energy than uprights, which open like refrigerators. If you're willing to manually defrost it, which takes about an hour no more than twice a year, you'll save money on electricity over the frost-free models. Stickers on the products will include an estimate of the yearly electrical usage and local cost to run. Newer models are generally much more energy efficient than freezers even a few years old, so be careful if you want to get one used; it may not be worth the initial savings.

Most good sales on meat take place in the fall. All that free summer grass dies, so fodder is more expensive in the winter. A freezer's handy to have to take advantage of the fall culling.

Time and space needs for nutritious meal planning are more a matter of priority than a true shortage for most people. It takes at least 20 minutes to go through the local fast food drive-through and a fair amount of space to store cake mixes and TV dinners, too, but when ingrained into routine, it doesn't seem difficult. Instead, make a healthier, money-saving habit of anticipating what the needs will be in the coming days and putting yourself in the most efficient position to fulfill them. Keep this up and, ultimately, running off to the store to get a box of brownie mix or to pick up a to-go pizza order will feel like the greater hassle, especially in light of the greater expense.

Chapter 7
The Price is Right

Quick, who has a better deal on cheddar cheese in a 10-mile radius from your house? Is three dollars a pound for London Broil a good deal, or not? What's a good per-ounce price for canola oil? Is $9.99 for 25 pounds of whole wheat flour a better deal than $8.59 for 20? You're blocking the aisle, already; hurry up!

As if our brains weren't taxed enough, there's the marketing tomfoolery to deal with. As food prices go up, food companies don't necessarily just raise the price on the same ol' box you've been buying for years. Nooooooo! They'll make the box a little smaller and hope you don't notice. Or they'll keep the box exactly the same size and just put less food in it, again counting on you not to check the fine print where it says "Net Wt." Don't get me started on how real food is rapidly being replaced with cheaper fillers that do humans no good at all, but keep bulk where nutrition used to be. It's a safe bet that the only thing truly "improved" when you see that word on the packaging is the food company's bottom line. My point is, you can't walk in "unarmed" to a supermarket and expect to spend wisely. MBA students spend whole semesters learning how to do this sneaky stuff.

How are you going to know you're spending wisely if you don't keep track of product prices? To make the most informed buying decisions, you need to know the following information:

- A list of products you routinely buy.
- Non-sale prices for those products, by package size and store.
- Sale prices for products, and dates purchased, so you'll know if sales are cyclical.
- Per-unit prices for products, such as by the pound, ounce, gallon, etc.

There is no way anyone could memorize all that information for even five products, let alone the dozens that the typical family buys, so you need a brain-assist or you're going to goof and spend more than is necessary.

A price tracking system should not be complicated or you won't use it, properly, or at all. The objective here is to know at a glance if what you're buying is cheaper than where you could get it somewhere else. The good news is that there are various ways to do this, and none of them are that difficult to make or maintain.

The first step for any system is to devise a way to find a product listing quickly. Some people just alphabetize their whole list and that's the end of it. Let me recommend that you divide your list by categories. Why? Because, most of the time, within the categories are the whole gamut of acceptable substitutes for any one item. So, if you have say, a "Fruit" category and grapes spike in price, it's nice to have apples right close by, since that's where you're likely to check next. You can nest these categories into finer sub-categories if you want to, but eschew complexity wherever possible.

Some people keep little 3-ring binders with handwritten records in them to keep track of all the prices for things they buy, and the stores where the item is available. Usually, with this system, there'd be tabs for the categories, and a page devoted to each item therein. Thus, our smart shopper would open up to the "Baking" tab, find the "Flour, White, All-Purpose" page and compare the price in front of him with those he's seen at other stores. The beauty of this system is that it's simple, available, and can be instantly updated. The only extra work involved is the rare page replacement when the old one fills up with obsolete data. The big downside is that if you accidentally leave it in your cart, years' worth of meticulous data collection is gone for good and you have to start from scratch.

Another system that solves the "theft or loss" problem, at least if you back up frequently, is just a simple spreadsheet list. A snippet of one example would be something like this:

Category	Item	Price	Qty	Unit	P/U	Where	Date
Baking							
	bk pwdr	8.59	5	lbs	1.718	p&s	4/9/08
		9.99	5	lbs	1.998	c	4/6/08
		10.89	5	lbs	2.178	s	7/8/08
	bk soda	9.99	10	lbs	0.999	c	9/9/08
	chc, unswt	4.99	3	lbs	1.663	hh	10/3/08
	chc chips	2.59	12	oz	0.215	c	1/3/07
	flour, white	4.79	25	lbs	0.191	s&f	8/8/08
	molasses	2.99	24	oz	0.124	s&f	8/8/08

The advantages of this system are that the per-unit calculations are automatically done for you, the information for each item is across one line; and should the printed copy be lost, the computer copy is still available at home. Note that baking powder has multiple line entries, one for each store price. The disadvantage is that the data has to be updated twice, once on paper at the store and once on the computer.

Ideally, if you have an electronic organizer, also known as a personal data assistant or smart phone, there should be a software program to keep the data straight. This would be ideal because any information you input from the store can be synchronized with the computer without having to retype it there. Well, I've been looking and so far I've seen products that will keep track of items and their prices usually don't keep the other pertinent information like quantities, unit prices, or store names. There are just straight database programs that let you make up your own fields, more in keeping with a spreadsheet. However, in most cases the display screen is so painfully tiny, setting up the price list would be difficult, unless you can do it on your computer first and then download it to the PDA. I haven't found a good one for my operating systems yet, but keep an eye out for yours. Until then, though the display is a little scrunched, some PDA's can download and display spreadsheets.

Again with the grumbling about how much time this will take! Really, it's not that bad.

- First, find your receipts from the last few weeks of shopping, or shop for a few weeks and save the receipts carefully.
- Step Two: Determine which system will work best for you and set up your titles, subheadings, basic organization.
- Step Three: Enter in as many items per category that you can remember that you buy.
- And finally, consult your receipts and fill in as much information as you can.

This'll take an hour; two, tops. And the money you'll save by being able to reliably buy food at the best prices available will more than pay for your time.

Still kvetching about all the time and effort needed to work out the best food options for your family? Let's put this into a little perspective. Who has a "bad boss" story? Me, too.

Once upon a time, when I was in college and finding myself very low on funds, I spied a "Help Wanted" sign in yonder flower shop window. Since I was a veteran of mostly food-service and house-cleaning jobs, the chance to work with clean, sweet-smelling flora much appealed to me, so I presented myself to the shop owner and, after a pleasant interview, was hired on the spot and told to report the very next day to the manager in charge.

The following morning, I arrived a few minutes early. The manager was on the phone taking down an order; she gave me a brief "welcome" smile, which I returned. So far so good! Well, I wanted to make that good first impression, to look eager and ready to work, so I glanced around, grabbed a broom and began sweeping the floor.

The phone call ended, and I barely had time to look up before the manager had covered the distance between us in a single bound. Her face was purple with rage. With a throbbing vein in her neck keeping time, she fumed, "Just WHAT are you DOING?!?"

Words failed me. I mean, there I was, standing there holding a broom, moving the dirt on the floor into a small pile; did she think this was an interpretive dance? Fortunately, the question was rhetorical. "I don't pay YOU to THINK! YOU do as you are TOLD, and NOTHING else! UNDERSTAND?!?"

I needed that job. I was just about broke, living on a can of chili a day, and the next trimester's fees were coming up. Without this job, I'd be dropping out of school and living in my car. This was no time for pride. "I- I'm sorry! What would you like me to do?" I asked in a small, submissive voice.

The manager blinked a couple of times. She hadn't thought about that. Finally, she looked at the floor. "Finish sweeping," she huffed, spun on her heel and walked away. Thus began probably the best day I had working for that manager.

I have some great boss stories, too. In fact, by the time I quit after our first baby was born, I absolutely loved my job, that manager and most of the other bosses I'd had since college. By then I was a software engineer, collecting raises and promotions left and right. What I liked best about my occupation was that I was paid to think. Naturally, when I went on the "Mommy Track," I made sure that I still "paid" myself to think, only this time it was in the area of savings. This turned out to be rather lucrative, compared to our spending habits before, and our standard of living, if anything, went up.

Invest time and intellect to make positive changes. The money you'll save by strategic thinking and planning your food expenditures will put you much, much closer to being your own boss.

Chapter 8
A Little Math Goes a Long Way

Relax. No logarithms or cosines will be harmed in your calculations of food values. The math we need to do is simple, but necessary, to see how our choices can make a big difference in nutrition and what's left in your wallet at the end of the month.

Let's look at the calculating the cost of food first, by looking at the cost of feeding the typical family for breakfast. I just saw a big box of Frosted Mini Wheats™ on sale for $2.50 for an 18-ounce box; that is about as cheap as I can get any cereal. That box will last my family about a morning, so that's $2.50 per breakfast for cereal. That doesn't seem so expensive, right? Well, let's do the numbers.

Compare and contrast boxed cereal with basic rolled oats, that I bought in bulk for $.36 a pound. It takes 3 cups to feed my whole family in the morning, with leftovers, which is .6 pounds, or about $.22. Add a generous amount for cinnamon sugar and the energy to boil water, and that brings it up to, say $.35.

Assuming all other factors, like the amount of milk and fruit consumed, is the same, our family saves $2.15 each morning we have the oatmeal instead of the cereal. Or, put another way, boxed cereal costs five times the amount of regular oatmeal. Once we do the math, that boxed cereal is looking expensive!

We also make our own waffles. Calculating the cost for this meal is a bit more tedious, but still not rocket science. If you know how much you paid initially for your ingredients, it's just basic math to calculate the price of each portion used. This big batch of waffles lasts us about five mornings:

- 4 cups white flour
- 4 cups whole wheat flour
- 2 cups oil
- 7 cups milk
- 8 eggs
- .25 cup sugar
- 16 teaspoons baking powder
- 2 teaspoons salt

White flour costs me $.18 a pound, but how many cups is that? Appendix A has a handy conversion chart for weight and volume for most common baking ingredients. Consulting the chart, it turns out that 4 cups is 1.2 pounds, so that's $.22. Whole wheat is $.36 a pound, and 4 cups totals $.43. I got 1.25 gallons of oil for $7.59. A gallon is 16 cups, 1.25 gallons is therefore 20 cups. And two cups works out to $.76. Nonfat milk is about $2.50 right now, but I still have some powdered milk I got that makes a gallon for $1.50. Seven sixteenths of $1.50 is $.66. Eggs are $2 a dozen, or $1.33 for the recipe. One-fourth of a cup of sugar is .12 pounds, or .12 of $.40 or about $.04. My baking powder was $8.59 for 5 pounds or 2.27 kilograms. According to the box, a quarter teaspoon is 1 gram, so I'm using .064kg for this recipe. 2.27 kilograms divided by .064kg reveals that I'm using 1/35th of $8.59 or about $.25 of baking powder. Salt is practically negligible since I buy it 25 pounds at a time for I think $5, so let's add a penny to be sure. Now add it all up, and five days' worth of waffles for the family comes to: $3.70, or $.74 a day.

We also make French Toast, toast with scrambled eggs, pancakes, bread pudding, muffins, granola and fritters, all of which when we do the math, we see this saves us as least $1.50 a day versus digging into a box of the cheapest cold cereal we can find. It's generally healthier, too.

Now for the fun part of this math exercise, also known as "The

Point." What is the savings for a year's worth of homemade breakfasts over cold store-bought cereal in cold, hard cash? 365 X $1.50 = $547.50. We can take the kids skiing for a couple of weekends just on what we save from breakfast.

Yes, calculating meal costs can be time-consuming, so don't reinvent the wheel calculating the cost of each ingredient all over again for every recipe. Instead, put your basic baking ingredients into a spreadsheet like this:

Ingredients Costs						
Ingredient	Qty Bought	Unit	Price	Price/Cup	Tablespoon	Teaspoon
white flour	25	lbs	4.5	$0.054	$0.003	$0.001
wheat flour	25	lbs	9	$0.108	$0.007	$0.002
oil	1.25	gal	7.59	$0.380	$0.024	$0.008
dry milk	10	gal	15	$0.094	$0.006	$0.002
white sugar	25	lbs	10	$0.200	$0.013	$0.004
bk pwdr	5	lbs	8.59	$0.842	$0.053	$0.018
salt	25	lbs	5	$0.100	$0.006	$0.002

To work out the price per cup, divide the price by the quantity and then multiply by the weight of volume needed. So, to figure out the price per cup of the white flour, it's the cell with 4.5 in it, divided by the cell with 25 in it, times .3 because a cup of white all-purpose flour is .3 of a pound. Viola! Each cup of white flour is about five and a half cents. If it goes up in price, just enter the new price in the appropriate place, and the formula will recalculate. Now print this out and stick it to the inside of your baking cabinet for a quick reality-check.

Taking the time to figure out the math is important if you want to know exactly how much you're spending to feed your family with the meal choices you make. Consider it a "pep talk" to keep you going when you see that the savings is not at all trivial. It'll also give you a new, almost-violent antipathy toward those frozen store-bought waffles, "instant" oatmeal, breakfast bars and other "convenience" foods that in reality are making you work longer hours to afford. And don't get me started on those pressurized cans of premade waffle batter!

Speaking of math, someone's going to gripe that time in the morning, or lack thereof, is a quantity that I should factor into my equations. I sympathize, but that's where a bit of planning comes in. Waffles, French toast and breakfast muffins can be made ahead during the weekend. Just freeze them. To use, pry them apart and either microwave or toast. Kids and hurried adults can handle that much work in the morning. The eggs can be scrambled, covered and refrigerated overnight, then cooked in five minutes while you're still in your pajamas. The oats can be measured and set on the counter, ready to dump in as soon as the water boils. Lay it all out when your brain is still working the night before, so you just have to add heat when you get up.

Strictly speaking, the main point of taking the time to work out this math is largely academic. Spending the time and math on the price book is much more important, if your time needs prioritization. If you bought the ingredients for the cheapest you could find, then at least 95% of the time, homemade will beat out its store-bought equivalent, and it'll be healthier to boot. Working out the math is mostly for self-gratification; a pep talk if you're tempted to go out or buy a frozen dinner.

Oh, and if you want to share your new-found knowledge, be sure to pick your audience. I once volunteered to bring treats for my son's Kindergarten, so I made my usual chocolate-chip cookie contribution that's always a crowd-pleaser. Another mother saw that it was home-baked and marveled that I took the time to do it. Without even thinking, I blurted out, "Well, this way it's only four cents per cookie." She gave me that bland "must move on before this nerd thinks we're friends" smile and walked away as quickly as politeness would allow. Working out the math and discovering that you're paying a dime to everyone else's dollar may bring great personal satisfaction, but you may need to keep that knowledge to yourself.

Chapter 9
Fruit Fetish

Y ou're having a quiet weekend afternoon at home, minding your own business. Suddenly, there's a knock at the door. Fear plucks at your heart. Not again! Surely the ordeal is over. You cautiously venture to the peephole on your door. Aaack! It's her! It's the neighbor with the hyper-prolific apple tree, and she's got another full grocery bag of Granny Smiths. The eyes of your children widen in fear as they scurry away in search for places to hide. Thinking of the next round of apple pork, apple sauce, apple pie, scrambled eggs with apples, apple chip cookies, etc., you and your spouse briefly consider making a break for it too, but then you sigh deeply and open the door. With smiles a bit too wide, you thank your kind neighbor for her incredible generosity . . . again.

The wise king had it right. "To everything, there is a season."[14] And when some fruits and vegetables are in season, your "cup runneth over." [15] And your pantry. And your garage. And your front porch. It is said that August is the only month small town residents lock their doors . . . to keep zucchini out.

---

[14] Ecclesiastes 3:1 KJV
[15] Psalm 23:5 KJV Both scriptural references are completely out of context, of course. Just trying to be funny.

There is something that can be done with all this ripe, cheap, abundant food. That's right, you can can it! Basically, this is the process of heating a food until any possible harmful microbes are killed, then vacuum-sealing it to keep more microbes out. So long as the seal holds, which can be years, the food will be perfectly edible.[16] It is the ultimate in "shelf stable" food, no freezer required.

Canning is amazingly easy, and equipment needs are few. You'll need a book on the subject, and there are many. You also need a big pot that can hold enough water to cover the jars with an inch of water, the jars, as well as the lids and rings. These latter three items at least are available in most grocery stores. Lids are flat disks that go over the mouth of the jar. Rings screw onto the top of the lid and jar, which squeezes the lid to the jar and seals it.[17] Everything but the lids are reusable, so once you acquire the equipment, the capital outlay is very little to can year after year.

So you mention to your friends that you're thinking about defending yourself against this summer's onslaught by taking up canning. Someone in your circle shudders delicately and makes dark references to botulism. To be sure, botulism is no joke. The bacterium Clostridium botulinum creates a nerve toxin that causes paralysis that often leads to death through respiratory failure. This microbe is commonly found in soil. Even more sinister, the toxins survive boiling temperatures. Suddenly your enthusiasm for home canning begins to wane.

Relax. First, the incidence of botulism in the U.S. is extremely low, fewer than two hundred cases a year, and only a very small fraction of those cases has anything to do with improper home canning. There's more good news, too. "Acid foods" prevent botulism by creating an environment too hostile for the bacteria to thrive. With the basic equipment you have, you'll be canning

Low-acid foods like green beans, meats and corn have to be canned under pressure. Most recipes require the food to endure 90 minutes at 10 pounds of pressure to ensure that the food can be stored safely.

---

[16] Though in some instances, it will discolor over time.
[17] Once heated in boiling water, the lid seals so tightly to the jar that some old-timers remove the rings to reuse once the jar is cool.

exclusively acid foods.

Acid foods are just that. Their pH is low enough, either in the food itself or in acid added to the jar, to prevent botulism. You can very safely can most fruits, tomatoes and pickles. Canning is no more difficult than following any basic recipe, and not all that time-consuming. Every year, my mother and I can enough chutney, apple butter and pie filling for the next year for both our families, as well as for a few gifts, in one marathon session of about eight hours.

There is one catch: Canned foods lose some nutrition during processing and storage. When some vitamins are exposed to light and heat, which happens when food is canned, they can degrade somewhat. Canned is almost never as good as fresh. (I say "almost" because in the case of tomatoes, lycopene, a really good antioxidant, is enhanced by cooking.) Frozen foods, while not being as good as just-picked, usually retain more nutrition than canning, too, but who has all that freezer space? Also, the sugar or salt content of the food will likely be higher than fresh. Canned food is very good for adding some interesting variety to an otherwise nutritious but slightly dull meal. Especially in the early spring, before the artichokes and snap peas are going full blast, our canned stuff breaks up the monotony of all those winter root vegetables nicely.

Another advantage of canning is that you're doing most of the work of preparing the food all at once, and later effort will be minimal. Should unexpected company arrive, I can get a pie in the oven in about 5 minutes, by dumping a quart of canned filling into a simple crust. Homemade spaghetti sauce just needs to be heated up to use with pasta, or not, to spread on pizza crust. In the doldrums of late Winter, when most "fresh" fruit is a week old from being shipped across the world and costs as much as my first car, I serve canned apricots as a side dish to liven things up a little.

Another area where canning surplus goods can save you money is by using them for gifts. I have a sister-in-law who routinely makes different interesting flavors of vinegar, jams, jellies and salsas to give away for various occasions, which are much appreciated by the

Make a point to casually mention to others that you like to can. You'll often receive supplies from retired folks who don't have kids to feed anymore.

recipients, myself included.

There's just something satisfying about inspecting row after row of jars, filled with colorful and interesting flavors, all at the ready like little soldiers defending us against high food prices. Canning a cheap or free surplus allows you not to miss a golden opportunity to save money on your food bill. It's yet another arrow in the whole quiver of strategies aiming for the cheapest way to feed our families nutritiously.

Chapter 10
Feast and Friends

I made a joke about the kindly neighbor bringing bags of apples around, but it's exactly that kind of cooperative living among others that efficiently distributes excess food, reduces waste, and builds community. Oh, and it saves a pile of money, too.

Every year, I start my tomatoes and peppers from seed right after Christmas, and repot them as they grow. Once they're big enough and the weather is kind enough to let them go into the ground, I invariably realize that I have way more than we can use, so I send them off to as many "good homes" as I can find. This same story plays out all through the Spring with many of my other plants, too. It's not a big effort for me, but several other families benefit and often grow bigger, better fruits and vegetables from my seedlings than I do, sigh.

One of my friends is an avid flower gardener, always trying new colors and fragrances, and every couple of years finds herself with more plastic nursery pots than she'd like, so she brings them by. This keeps my seed starting and distribution operation going very cheaply, so I am always grateful.

Another friend is somewhere close to her eighties now, and quite done with canning, so she gave me all her old supplies. I made sure she got a couple of her jars back, filled of course. Turns out she just loves caramel spiced apple butter and you just can't find that kind of thing in stores.

Yet another friend of mine owns a dump truck. In exchange for my finding a good place to get composted manure cheaply, he offered to bring me a large portion of the haul. So, I talked to a stable owner who was only too happy to get rid of some of her large pile. We showed up with a nice selection of garden products, canned and fresh, which surprised and delighted her. We'll be welcome again.

Yes, I get armloads of fruits and vegetables every year from various friends, relatives and neighbors. Apples. Pomegranates. Zucchini. And I give armloads away. Oranges. Lemons. Tomatoes. Cucumbers. Adam Smith is as right today as he was in his book "The Wealth of Nations" 400 years ago. Trade makes winners of all the participants.

These stories are but a few ways in which having a network of caring people around me has helped immensely in providing me wonderful, low-cost food. A few ideas for your own:

1. Don't keep score. This isn't about manipulating people into getting what you want. You should genuinely want to help others, and want them to genuinely want to help you. Your surplus was going to rot anyway, so even if you don't get anything in return, you've avoided waste. If you find yourself in a one-sided relationship over time, however, it's perfectly all right to step back. Your efforts may not be fully appreciated and would be better served elsewhere. Some people just don't like to play with others, and you can't make them.

2. Do make a point to reciprocate as soon as possible in some way when someone has been generous to you, especially if this person is new to the "network." This lets him know that you both appreciate his thinking of you and that you want to maintain the cooperative relationship with him, which will be of mutual benefit.

3. Food-savings cooperation does not always take material form. Before you head out to a store, call a friend you see often and ask if there's anything you can pick up for her

while you're there. Since gasoline is so expensive and time is precious, too, this will be most appreciated.

4. If you find a good deal on a perishable item that has to be purchased in a bulk size beyond your capacity to consume it in time, get on the phone and find someone willing to split it with you. Both parties will benefit.

> A network of sharing friends is great for more than just food of course! You'll find one ready-made by going to: http://freecycle.org and choosing the group nearest you. Be sure to follow their by-laws!

5. This one's tricky, but it's often not a good idea to refuse something offered, even if you can't/won't use it. If someone shows up at your doorstep with a food that won't work for you, smile sweetly and graciously accept the gift, especially if this is a new giver. You can always "gift" it elsewhere, and the giver will likely keep you in mind if he has a surplus of something else down the line. If you decline, he might take that as rejection, and you've lost a member of your network for good. However, if he asks if you'll use it, be honest. Or if this surplus is the "gift that keeps on giving," you may want to come clean, diplomatically, of course. The idea is to welcome all comers into the fold, and not discourage anyone.

6. Information is valuable, too. Once you learn a new skill, offer to teach others. If you get wind of a killer sale, pass it on.

I'm not a Barbra Streisand fan or anything, but people who need people *are* the luckiest people in the world. I share my "wealth" with others who don't necessarily share my faith, my political leanings or really have anything else in common with me, but they all understand the mutual benefit there is in helping each other. It's hard to quantify the exact amount of money and time you'll gain by doing this, but it's well worth your investment.

Let's go back to that peaceful afternoon when the apples arrive.

You fling open the door in welcome. "Oh, Mrs. O'Leary! " you cry. "How nice to see you! Wow! More apples, thank you! I wanted to drop by later to give you these." You hand her a quart of apple pie filling and a pint of apple butter. A very pleased Mrs. O'Leary stammers her thanks. Feeling the heft of this grocery bag, you decide that you should pass on some of the largesse to one of your friends who has several children, and you can make a batch of dried apple chips from the rest. They're great in salads. You'll make sure to mention that to Mrs. O'Leary when you take her some.

Part II
Use It or Lose It

 Bringing the food into the house is one side of the coin, using it efficiently is the other. Half-price food is no savings if half of it is thrown away. (Would you have cared about it more if you'd paid full price?) There are also moral considerations to wasted food, especially now that food prices have spiked so dramatically in the last couple of years that nearly one billion people in the world face severe shortages.

Using up your leftovers also saves gas and electricity, as well as the time to go buy more food. Let's also not forget that leftovers by definition are food in which you've already invested effort and energy to prepare, which on the one hand will be lost if you toss them, but on the other hand, will likely make it much quicker and easier to use again – leftovers are fast food!

The good news is that finishing off that flotsam and jetsam from the past few days doesn't have to mean that you'll have to eat the same reheated meal over and over until it's finally gone, or forms a crust too hard to chew. In fact, pre-cooked foods are the perfect ingredients for a wide  variety of interesting, healthful and delicious new entrées. In this second half of the book, you'll find exactly the kind of "flexipes," that is, flexible recipes you need to get your money's worth out of your food.

Just for laughs, you can hear the late George Carlin's hilarious take on leftovers in his "Icebox Man" routine at: http://www.youtube.com/watch?v=KxAg-mBpE6o

Chapter 11
Boning Up and Taking Stock

There's a place for those limp stalks of celery, those carrots that can bend in half without breaking, those dry-looking onions with brown around the edges, meat scraps, peelings. Not only are they still useful, but in their new capacity, they take on a fancy new French name: mirepoix, pronounced "mihr-pwah." This is the high-falutin' word for chopped-up stuff that flavors broth.

Making good stock, also known as bouillon or broth, is simple. If you have a slow cooker, plug it in, and fill it about half-full with liquid. Plain water doesn't have to be the only choice for steeping past-their-prime vegetables. Reserve the water that turned a deep, rich green when you steamed that spinach for dinner the other night, and add it to the pot. Liquid from canned foods, flat beer and wine also give broth a nice "head start." Now, chop up those geriatric vegetables and drop them in the pot. (The general agreement in cooking circles is that two parts onion to one part each of the other ingredients makes the nicest flavor.) Let simmer all day or night. Without a slow cooker, this can be done on the stove top with a little more supervision.

A great time to make stock is when you're boning meat or cutting up a chicken carcass and have the whole back and giblets left over. Plop it in your pot, add a couple of teaspoons of vinegar to the water[18], let simmer all night, and in the morning, the remaining meat will be falling off of the bones. Strain to save the liquid, then pick out all the good meat and toss the rest. You now have a wonderful broth and some fully-cooked meat ready to be put to good use.

What's so wonderful about broth, anyway? This basic stock can enhance the nutrition and taste of meals in a large number of ways. A few are detailed below.

It's good as, well, broth. Curl up with a good book, some crackers and a mug of hot broth to warm yourself inside and out on a cold day.

Soup. This is probably the most common use for stock. In the morning, pour your bouillon into a slow cooker or a pot on the stove. From here, you can assemble just about any kind of soup you'd like. Soaked beans, vegetables from the garden, dried split peas, lentils, barley and other grains, pre-cooked meats, uncooked meats that aren't too fatty, spices and more can all go in to simmer all day long, filling your house with the intoxicating smell of a warm, inviting home. If you want noodles, don't add the dried pasta until about half an hour before serving, or they'll be mush. Likewise, precooked vegetables don't need the all-day treatment, but can certainly join the soup a little while before serving. Also, salt can prevent beans from softening; add that seasoning at the last minute. Other than those few precautions, this is a no-fail, great use for leftovers, anything-goes type of filling meal which should definitely be on your menu often.

Chowder. It's amazing how simply thickening a soup changes its character so dramatically. There are two main ways to turn a simple broth-based soup into a chowder. The first is a puree. Remove at least a third of the solid ingredients in the soup, pour into a blender and run it until the mixture is smooth. Then pour the puree back into the soup. The second way to thicken a soup to make a chowder is the last-minute inclusion of half-and-half or cream. Don't let either simmer too long or the heat will curdle them. Of course, with this last method you've added fat and calories along with taste, but what a rich addition it is.

Stew. Like chowders, stews thicken a basic soup, but with a starch and/or a fat. Flour and butter are classic soup thickeners for stew. For every four cups or so of soup, mix about three or four

---

[18] You won't taste the vinegar but it will leach calcium from the bones into the water; more nutrition for you.

tablespoons of flour with an equal amount of butter (or fat drippings) in a saucepan over medium heat until bubbly, then add liquid from the soup. Stir well, and when the mix thickens, add it back to the rest of the soup, and stir again. If the soup still needs thickening, you can make a "putty ball" with equal parts butter and flour, and just drop it in.[19]

Corn starch is also highly-prized for its coagulant properties. To thicken four cups of soup, add two tablespoons of corn starch to half a cup of *cold* water and shake or stir vigorously until dissolved. Add to soup and stir. Do not add corn starch directly to hot soup or it will form unappetizing lumps.

Potato water, that is water that potatoes boiled in, with perhaps a bit of mashed potato has sufficient starch to thicken stews, or you can buy powdered potato starch to do the job. Many stews have potatoes in them already, which makes them more dense as a matter of course. Other starches that naturally make a stew more "hearty" through their thickening properties include many grains like bulgur, rice, barley and the like.

Arrowroot is a flour made from the root of the manioc plant. No, I didn't know what that was, either, but it's native to the tropics of the American continents, which is a fun fact you should know to make yourself more interesting at dinner parties. Also, it has twice the thickening power of regular white wheat flour, and does not cloud the water it thickens. So there you have it.

All in all, what distinguishes a stew from a soup is the near gravy-like consistency of the liquid around the other ingredients. While soup is often relegated to single-course or light-lunch status, often necessitating a bread to fill out the meal, stews have that "full rib-sticking dinner" swagger about them. A little starch makes all the difference in our sense of fullness. I was going to make a joke here about stuffed shirts and the starch in them, but I'll repress myself.

Sauces. Now that you can make the gravy for a stew, you can do the same thing to broth by itself to pour over meat, potatoes or vegetables that just need that little "something" to make them more interesting. Sauté a few finely chopped onions and/or other vegetables in butter to add texture and flavor to your sauce and you'll

---

[19] This is called "manny butter," an anglicized-version of the French beurre manié. Now practice putting this fact into the form of a question for your star turn on Jeopardy.

likely have rave reviews at the table. Broth can also be the basis for white sauce and its many variations. Any basic cookbook will have instructions for white sauce and the "small sauces" that can be made from it; it's like the Swiss Army Knife of culinary complements.

Braises. This is the liquid in which a meat simmers and steams for long periods of time. Chicken Fricassee and Pot Roast are two meats that are braised, for example. Of course the meat contributes to its own broth in this case, but starting with a broth only improves the result.

In Recipes. Almost anywhere a liquid is used in a dish, broth can do the job for a boost in flavor. This applies to everything from breads to chili to stuffing to risottos.

It's a stretch, but when I think of the ingredients in stock, I'm reminded of the arboreal protagonist in Shel Silverstein's "The Giving Tree." Even when she's given practically all she has to The Boy, she still has a stump for sitting on. Most of the things that go in stock likewise seem beyond usefulness, but in fact have one last good purpose. Making stock is one of those activities that has no down side; it only costs pennies to make, hands-on time is less than ten minutes, it uses up food that would otherwise be wasted, and forms the basis for many different kinds of nutritious meals. Make the delicious and very lucrative habit of starting stock whenever you're cutting up meat and/or when the veggies are making a liar out of the "crisper" drawer in the refrigerator.

Chapter 12
Strange Breadfellows

I keep reading about these new "smart" appliances that are going to make all our lives so much simpler. The high I.Q. refrigerator is supposed to know when you're running low on milk and call the store for delivery. That'd be okay, if it would also first make price comparisons and haggle to get the delivery charge waived. What I'd really like, however, is a refrigerator that could come up with recipes based on all the odds and ends therein.

Here's a recipe I'm sure GE won't ever program (Read in robot voice):

TAKE ¾ CUP OF MILK THAT SOME KID FORGOT TO DRINK THIS MORNING AND YOU DIDN'T CATCH IN TIME, ADD 1 ¾ CUP OF CHICKEN SOUP BROTH FROM THE OTHER NIGHT AND WARM SLIGHTLY IN MICROWAVE. IN THE MEANTIME, IN STANDING MIXER BOWL, PUT 1 TABLESPOON YEAST, 2 TABLESPOONS VITAL WHEAT GLUTEN, ¾ TABLESPOON SALT, ¼ C OIL, AND 2 TABLESPOONS BROWN SUGAR. ADD SIX EGG YOLKS LEFT OVER FROM MAKING A BIRTHDAY CAKE FIVE DAYS AGO, AND THE 1/3 CUP MASHED SWEET POTATOES FROM SOMETIME LAST WEEK

THAT MIRACULOUSLY HASN'T GONE BAD YET. NOW
KNEAD IN WHOLE WHEAT FLOUR, ~7CUPS, UNTIL IT
LOOKS LIKE BREAD DOUGH. LET RISE. SHAPE. LET
RISE AGAIN. BAKE. SERVE TO FAMILY WITH STRAIGHT
FACE.

In Ulm, Germany, there's a whole museum dedicated to bread
and its six thousand year human history. It was there that I realized
that bread takes on more forms than there are people to bake them.
So long as the proportions of the basic types of ingredients are not
too far out of whack, you can make good bread out of any number of
foods.

Let's look at what categories of ingredients make up your basic
yeast loaf.

1. There's yeast. That can be active dry, cake[20], or a strain from
   some kind of starter, of which there are thousands.
2. There's flour. Somehow, gluten needs to be involved to make
   the dough rise with the action of the yeast, but barring that,
   just about any kind of flour will work. Wheat flour needs
   about 14% protein content, which is the gluten. For optimal
   rising, at least three quarters of the flour needs to be a high-
   gluten wheat variety.[21]
3. There's liquid. Water works. So does milk, broth, beer, juice,
   water left over from boiling potatoes (called "potato water")
   or pasta, and so forth. Many bread books caution that when
   dissolving the yeast, to do so in a little bit of warm (110F or
   43C) water first, then use any other liquid for the rest. We
   want our yeast awake and healthy, ready to get to work.
4. There's something to inhibit the action of the yeast somewhat
   so the bread doesn't rise too quickly and turn to mush.
   Usually, this inhibitor is salt, but in salt-free recipes, one can
   use half the yeast and watch the bread carefully, though it still
   won't turn out as well. I have also read that cinnamon and
   garlic are among ingredients that can slow yeast down.

[20] It's almost impossible to find yeast in this form anymore, but no one really
misses it.
[21] You can bake gluten-free bread, made from grains like rice. You have to use 2-3
times more yeast, and do some other tricks to make it work. Run a search for
recipes on the Internet.

Those four ingredients are the bare minimum to make some kind of bread. Commonly added to make yeast loaves:

5. A fat of some sort helps the loaf brown nicely and keeps it from drying out as quickly. Fats include anything rendered from animals, any kind of vegetable oil, shortening, or butter.

6. Sugar gives the yeast more to eat than the carbohydrates in the flour, makes for better browning and of course sweeter taste in the bread. Sugar can be honey, molasses, brown or white sugar, et cetera/

7. Eggs add a richness to the flavor and texture of bread.

Make bread with the first four ingredients, and you'll have a perfectly passable loaf. French bread and sourdough are both primarily made this way. Add the next three and you'll have a softer, richer, more flavorful

> Make sure the water used doesn't contain chlorine or chloramine like many city supplies do, which will kill your yeast. Filtered water from the tap will generally work, as will bottled, boiled or distilled.

result. But true uniqueness comes with what you do next! Take care not to overwhelm the rest of the ingredients, but go through your refrigerator and your pantry and see what you can add. Some suggestions include herbs and spices, cooked grains like rice, oatmeal and tapioca; nuts, purees, and mashed or finely chopped fruits and vegetables. Do determine ahead of time if you're going in a sweet or a savory direction and choose additions accordingly.

Technique in bread-making is key, as well. If it's active dry, dissolve the yeast in a bit of slightly-warmer-than-lukewarm (110F, 43C) water for a few minutes until it's a bit bubbly. If it's sourdough, you'll need about a cup of the starter at room temperature. Toss in the rest of the ingredients, except for the flour. Adding the flour is the artful part of this venture. Start with half your flour all at once, then add the next quarter by cups. At this point, the dough should be firm enough that you can turn it out onto your pastry board and knead in the rest by degrees. If you have a mixer with a dough hook, and therefore don't have to knead by hand, add the last bit of your flour by quarter cupfuls, taking care that each addition is fully integrated into the dough before adding more. In either case, the result you're looking for is smooth and elastic, with a slightly moist, often described as "glossy" surface. If you lightly indent the dough, it'll spring back. Depending on what you added to the dough, it might be a little sticky; don't worry about that.

To knead by hand: Fold the dough in half, push down with the heels of your hands. Turn 90 degrees. Repeat. Keep doing this for about ten minutes. And feel the burn!

Cover with oiled plastic wrap or a damp towel and let rise in a warm place until about doubled in size, often in about 45 minutes under optimal conditions with active dry yeast, or a couple of hours with a starter. At this point, an indent won't spring back.

Divide the dough into however many loaves you'll make. To shape, push the dough down to about an inch high with your knuckles,

> You can put your dough out to rise in a tall, see-through plastic container with a rubber band around the outside to mark the beginning height. Then you'll know exactly when it's doubled.

fold into thirds, then roll together, pinching all the seams. Place in greased bread pan or on sheet seam side down and bake at around 350F for around 25 minutes for a normal-sized loaf, less for smaller.

The following is a guide to proportions of ingredients:

- Yeast: 1 tablespoon active dry or 1 cup starter for every 6 or so cups of flour (makes 2 loaves)
- Liquid: 2 – 2 1/4 cup, depending on moisture of additions. If using starter, 1 1/4 cup is usually enough.
- Fat: 1/4 cup
- Eggs: 2-3
- Sugar: 0 to 1/3 cup (more for sweet bread)
- Salt: 1 1/2teaspoon – 1 tablespoon
- Other: up to 1 1/2 cups
- Flour: 5 1/2 -7 cups, depending upon moisture of additions

Remember in Chapter One when I could only afford one package of commercial yeast, but I wanted to make breads for a whole week? Since yeast is alive, it can reproduce under the right conditions, so I can grow more before I use some, by simply dropping the package of yeast into a container with equal parts flour and water. By the next day, the yeast will have formed a bubbly mass; I'd stir it and wait for it to calm down to about pancake-batter consistency before using a portion of it. Add a little flour and water each day to the unused portion, both to keep it alive and to build up enough for the next batch. Yeast will thrive as long as it has something to eat. It will also get more sour-tasting over time, as symbiotic bacteria start to thrive and produce acid, which for those of us who like sourdough, this is a good thing.

You can use your sourdough starter indefinitely. Don't worry if it separates, just stir it. But if it grows mold, toss it and start over. Consult the Internet for other things you can do with sourdough starter: pizza dough, pancakes, tortillas, pot pies. . . The more frequently it is used, the better. If you're going to use it every other day or so, just keep it on the counter somewhere out of the way. But if you're only going to use it once or twice a week, slow down the action of the yeast by refrigerating it. If you need to put it into stasis while you go on vacation or a business trip, freeze it. Once thawed, it will likely resume activity. Do make sure that you bring your yeast back to room temperature before using it.

There are many strains of yeast and the lactobacilli that often live with them to metabolize and consume sugars from flour, and they all impart different flavors into bread. These microbes float freely around in the air and are also present on the surface of the grains that make breads. Thus, if you want to make a truly wild sourdough starter, you can mix water and flour into a dough and leave it out to pick up whatever's thriving in your local area. The bread you make will be very specific to your region. Give it to visitors as a souvenir! This also means that if I were more patient, I wouldn't need to spend that $.72 in Chapter One to get the commercial yeast to make starter.

Whatever yeast you use, good bread is a combination of ingredients and timely procedure. Problems can arise even if your proportions are fine, but your timing is off. Suppose you set your dough out to rise and forget all about it for hours. Your yeast has been very busy during all that time, so now your dough has lost most of its structure and cohesion, leaving you with a stringy, primordial-looking mass that you need to get rid of before it evolves and eats your family, right? Nah. Just change your dinner plans a bit, because once you dust that mess with flour and knead it a little, you've got the foundation for pizza crust, tortillas or pita bread. Even the most neglected dough is usually salvageable.

Simple instructions for how to cultivate your local yeast can be found at: http://www.exploratorium.edu/coo king/bread/recipe-sourdough.html

Bread is truly the staff of life, and most families eat a lot of some form of it, which means if you gain proficiency baking, you'll save money by not having to buy bread every week and also by using it to "soak up" some of your food odds and ends. I also find that I save money on snack foods, since my kids just love fresh baked bread. This chapter contains a broad description of the bread making process, but if you're truly new to baking, I highly recommend that you pick a basic recipe out of a book and make that for a few batches, until you can consistently turn out a good loaf. After that, enjoy the adventure of putting your leftovers to good use in a place no one's looking for them!

Chapter 13
Bean There, Done That

Beans should fire their publicist. To bad-mouth an accountant, call him a "bean counter." To bad-mouth a skinny person, call him a "string bean." A slang term for head is "bean." To divulge a confidence is to "spill the beans." Pythagoras, the philosopher and mathematician from the sixth century B.C. was famous also for his abstention from beans. And that British mute doofus? Mr. Bean, of course. In its profile of a "hungry" family, one magazine article dismissively mentioned that the mother was glumly standing over a pot of beans, as if this was just one step away from eating the front lawn.

Humble beans are very nutritious, a good source of protein[22], fiber, folate, calcium and iron. In fact, in any list of healthiest food that you can find, beans always rank in the top ten or twelve! They're low in fat. In their dried state, they take up little space in the pantry, and store indefinitely. And they're cheap. You can still get several varieties for less than a buck a pound. When prepared, that single pound easily becomes three pounds of cooked beans, enough to fill up six people. Both pre-soaked and cooked, they can be frozen for later use. Beans have such a neutral taste, they can be prepared in

---

[22] Serve with a grain like rice to complete the protein.

dozens of different ways and, most of the time, different kinds can be used interchangeably in recipes. Of course, they can also absorb plenty of leftovers along the way. For all these reasons, beans should be high on your list of low-cost, high-nutrition meal options.

And the downside? Well, there's the long preparation time. Beans need to be soaked in four times their volume of water, preferably for at least six hours, then rinsed well before simmering in new liquid for several hours before they're tender enough to taste good. You can speed up the first part by bringing the beans to a boil in your soak water then letting them sit for an hour.

Cooking beans sounds like a job for a slow cooker, all right. This is why it's very helpful to plan dinners ahead, and know what the dinner plan is for the next day by the night before. You'll have enough time to thaw stuff, soak beans and prepare some ingredients for tossing in the slow cooker the next morning. This is my personal favorite for cooking a bean meal, because it requires the least amount of effort on my part, fills the house with a delicious smell all day, uses less energy than using an oven, and it's ready whenever I feel like serving it.

There's a faster way to cook beans that I first came across in a reader's contribution to The Tightwad Gazette, which was a

> Soaking and rinsing your beans very well helps to alleviate that, uh, second downside to this food.

fantastic compendium of all ideas frugal that ran from 1990 to 1996. Someone submitted a way to pressure cook beans and rice in about 45 minutes, from start to finish! You need two metal or glass bowls, one small enough to fit in the cooker, but large enough to hold the second, smaller container. First, bring a cup of dry beans to a boil, then pour off the water, put the beans into the larger container and add two cups fresh water plus two tablespoons of oil. (The oil helps to keep the beans from foaming, which could clog the pressure valve.) Into the smaller container goes 1 cup of brown rice with 1½ cups of water. Place the smaller container on top of the beans in the larger container, then put foil over both. (Again, this is to help prevent clogging of the all-important pressure valve.) Pour an inch or so of water into the bottom of your pressure cooker, set the food ensemble inside, close it up, and turn on the heat. Your entrée, enough to feed four adults, is ready once the weight's been rocking steadily for about a half hour. Add spices and serve. This meal is faster and less work than a trip to McDonald's and barely costs a dollar.

As long as the spices are compatible, many leftovers and fresh vegetables can join your beans. Add cilantro and cumin for a Mexican direction, curry for Indian cuisine, tomato paste with basil and oregano for Italian, molasses and mustard powder for Boston Baked Beans, fennel and yogurt for Greek, maybe? And so on.

My personal favorite leftover-absorption-through-beans strategy is chili. One year, our Boy Scout district bought too many hamburgers and hotdogs for the last day of its Day Camp. I rescued some 30 pounds of grilled meat from going into the dumpster and stuck it in my freezer while I figured out what to do with it all. This was mostly cooked hamburger that had been sitting in the hot summer sun for over an hour until it was dried out. I knew I couldn't just microwave it, unless I was using it for shoe repair. For eating, I'd need to boil it back into edibility. This sounded like a job for chili!

When putting this meal together, I put my six cups of presoaked beans in first, so I'd know how much room is left in the slow cooker to add other odd and ends. I hacked away at several hard-rubber hamburgers until I got them into fork-sized morsels and tossed them in next before digging up an onion or two as well as whatever vegetables were ripe from the garden. Chopped into small enough pieces, many vegetables do a great job of adding color and interest to the bean landscape. If I'd had pre-cooked vegetables, I'd have chopped those into small pieces and stirred them in an hour or so before serving. In the back of the refrigerator, I found about a cup of pureed pumpkin and a pint or so of spaghetti sauce. Sure, why not? After stirring, I obviously needed some liquid to go with all this, so I mixed in enough chicken broth and tomato catsup to cover. Chili beans need chili powder, of course, so I tossed in a couple of tablespoons to start, with the promise to add more once I tasted it later. A little cumin always goes a long way, so I put in just a teaspoon or so. I turned the slow cooker on and walked away. Eight hours and some salt and spice adjusting later, this was a terrific meal that tasted even better after some had been frozen and served later.

Thanks to that one mistake, I had enough grilled meat for a year's worth of chilis, hamburger stews, split pea soups and pigs-in-a-blanket. To be honest, at the time, the meat didn't look like there was much of a second-life for it, but my Scotch heart couldn't bear to see that much food go to waste, and that's where knowing a few "flexipes" comes in handy.

Notice that my one slow cooker-full of chili, three meals' worth, with fresh vegetables and lots of meat cost me less than a dollar to feed my family for the evening. To do the same with convenience-food chili, which leaves something to be desired in both taste and nutrition, I would have had to spend somewhere around $12 to get six small cans, and probably would have wasted another three dollars' worth of food in unused leftovers. If all my dinners are five dollars cheaper than their pre-made store-bought counterparts, I save close to two grand in the course of a year. And that's just on dinner. We haven't even discussed breakfast, lunch and snacks.

You opened to the chapter on beans, and here you are getting a sermon. However, now is as good a place as any to discuss how attitude plays into meeting your money-saving goals in the areas of food, or anywhere else for that matter. Many people don't think saving a little here and there is worth all the "trouble." In the case of most leftovers, so much of the processing has already been done; the extra work is minimal to reuse them in something else. The knowledge of how to do it is really the missing link here, and the lack of understanding that the money saved is not just a pittance.

In the case of the meat, many couldn't stomach (pun intended) the idea of food meant for another purpose going to their own families, and so they wouldn't touch it. Likewise, many people have difficulty with the idea of "retooling" leftovers into new meals and just want to toss whatever doesn't get eaten that day, never mind what their mothers told them about children in Ethiopia. Thank goodness this isn't you, but you may have to gently re-educate people around you, and endure a few looks when you lug 30 pounds of cooked meat to your car. (I did try to share, honest!) Just hold your head up high and take the family to Hawaii for a week with the savings you'll accumulate this year.

Chapter 14
Totally Fried

The stock and bean chapters have largely covered ways to cook foods in liquid, which I admit I do often because I can usually chuck something in the slow cooker and forget about it all day when I'm otherwise busy or lazy, or busy being lazy. However, other ways of food preparation don't take that much more time and effort; preparations just take place closer to the dinner hour. Take frying, for example. This chapter details several methods of using up leftovers on your griddle or skillet.

Many meals that are fried actually require that the food be pre-cooked, as it won't be on the skillet long enough to heat fully all the way to the center, therefore leftovers are ideal for these applications. Also, the oil involved in many cases isn't more than one-eighth of an inch, so you're not adding as many calories to the mix as might be imagined. It is a good idea to use oils that can withstand high heat without smoking; canola and safflower are two that come to mind. Both are low in saturated fats as well. Below are some different frying methods.

Hash. Everyone's had hash browned potatoes; here, you're just adding food to it. Mix one part of some leftover food, preferably meat, with an equal amount of grated potato with a bit of something else, like onion or a veggie to add color. Fry in about an eighth of an inch of oil, turning once to cook both sides. The hash can be a single large one half inch thick pancake or shaped into individual portions for easier turning. Hash doesn't actually have to be fried; it can also be baked at 350-375F (176-191C) for 15 to 20 minutes.

Fritters. These are basically pancakes with food in them, which can be fruits, meats or vegetables. For every part of chopped food pieces that you intend to use, mix a half-part flour with a half-part water. Combine and season all the ingredients. Put the resultant batter in the refrigerator for at least an hour to allow it to get thick. You can pour off the liquid that separates out for thicker fritters. Add an egg or a couple of egg whites. (To make these really light, separate the egg and fold in the stiff egg white right before frying.) Fry these just like pancakes, in an eighth of an inch of hot oil and turning once. Serve right away.

Fritters are a perfect quick breakfast option. The first time I made these, I noticed after dinner one night that I had a about a quart of already-opened canned apricots, so I added in enough flour to make a good pancake batter and put it in the refrigerator. In the morning, once I rolled out of bed, I fired up the griddle and added 3 beaten eggs to the batter. Less than eight minutes later, I had about 30 dollar-sized fritters ready.

Fried Rice. If you have leftover rice and need dinner in the next ten minutes, this one's a good choice. Simply heat a couple of tablespoons of oil in a skillet, sauté an onion if you've got one, then throw in your precooked rice and anything else that will go: leftover beans, meats, veggies, whatever. Let everything brown nicely, then season to taste and serve. You can pour a little water in the bottom and cover to steam the last couple of minutes of cooking if your rice is a little dry.

Stir Fry. The stir fry was an invention borne of the high cost of energy, so it deserves a second look today. By the thirteenth century, the Chinese were running out of fuel for their cooking fires, so they cut their food small and fried it quickly, adding sauces along the way. Thus, the stir fry was born. This really works best with about a half-inch of oil in the bottom of a wok. Start with raw meat, coated with a batter or not, and cook until done through. Now add some onions and fry until browned. Finally, add fresh vegetables. Fry until slightly wilted, drain off excess oil, then turn down the heat. Now's a good time to add a sauce; either a sweet and sour or a simple teriyaki work fine. Thicken slightly, then cover and allow to steam and thicken some more for just a few minutes. Don't let your vegetables wilt into total mush; they're best with a little crunch. You'll find some pretty good sweet and sour recipes by running a search engine on-line, so you can tune them to what you have on hand. Serve immediately over rice. If you're about to protest that you don't see any mention of leftovers here, you got me. This dish really doesn't work well with most pre-cooked food, but it's low-cost, tasty, easy, fast, and uses a lot of vegetables with just a little meat or tofu, so if your garden is getting ahead of you, it's a good choice, even if leftovers aren't in the picture. Sue me.

Croquettes. If you can make a thick white sauce, which any basic cookbook will explain, then you can make croquettes. With meat and vegetables, these make an entrée, with fruits and other sweet ingredients, you can go in a more dessert-like direction. Take two parts leftovers, chopped small, and mix them with a very thick white sauce. Chill for a couple of hours in the refrigerator or an hour in the freezer. Shape into small patties no more than one and a half inches thick. Bread them and chill again for a half hour in the refrigerator, if possible. Now heat enough oil to float the croquettes. Once the oil is hot enough to make batter sizzle, say 375F (191C), lower as many as can comfortably fit in the oil. Brown them evenly. Serve hot. To be honest, I'm not a fan of these because the white sauce is more fat and carbohydrates than I want, and mine usually come out pretty greasy, not to mention that all that oil costs more than the ingredients. But, in the interest of full disclosure, croquettes are one way to disguise and use up leftovers.

Tempura. While we're on the subject of deep fat frying, tempura is another way to work with food, though like stir fries, it works more often with fresh food that needs to be used up than with leftovers. All the great things I said about stir fries applies here as well, it's cheap, easy, fast, uses up a lot of the garden harvest, tastes great... and one more advantage: it hides some of the less-popular vegetables, like egg plant or zucchini.

So, got beer? It's really good in tempura batter. Allow me to veer off topic for a moment and mention a few other cool things about beer, since people sometimes bring the stuff to our parties and then we have to figure out what to do with it. Beer makes for good liquid in pizza dough and fish batter. Use it in marinades and barbecue sauces. Pour a can into the slow cooker and add meat and spices for a really good pot roast. Beer Can Chicken uses the liquid for basting on the outside and steaming from inside, where the can is in the cavity of the chicken, propping up the carcass for even roasting. In the garden, pour a little beer into cups that are sunk into the ground, and slugs will drown in it by the dozens. Type "uses for beer" into a search engine and you'll have sites declaring it works for everything from shampoos to fertilizer. I've heard some people actually drink the stuff. Eeeww!

Getting back on the train of thought now, a basic tempura batter combines a cup of cold beer with a cup of flour and a little salt. Don't mix it too much and keep it really cold. In fact, some instructions insist that you put an ice cube in the middle of the batter. Search for "tempura batter recipes" on the Internet, and you'll find many, with varying numbers of ingredients and complexity. Cut your vegetables into longish and thin strips, dip into the batter and deep fry in 375F (191C) oil until golden brown. Any reasonably firm vegetable works great with this: potatoes, string beans, onions, carrots, etc. I wouldn't try this on more delicate vegetables like snow peas; they'll likely degrade into something floppy and unappetizing. You can also tempura quick-cooking meats like shrimp or fish. Blot the oil from the food and serve hot, with rice and soy sauce if desired.

Crepes. This is another dish perfect for leftovers as it cooks only long enough to melt cheese; therefore most of the food in it needs to be precooked. Crepes resemble fritters in that they have a pancake-like structure, but they are thinner and the food is not integrated into the crepe itself; rather, the crepe enfolds the food like a burrito. Crepes can be made for dessert or dinner; the difference is only in what it wraps. Here is a basic recipe for 15 ten-inch crepes.

Oil makes the crepes softer; butter, more crisp. Also, you'll need to add a bit more fat to the skillet every crepe or two to prevent sticking.

2 cups flour
4 eggs
1 cup each of milk and water

1/2 teaspoon salt

2 tablespoons melted butter

Whisk all the ingredients together until smooth and runny. Heat a thin coating of oil or butter on medium heat in your skillet until it's bubbly, then pour in about a quarter of a cup of the batter. Immediately turn the skillet until most of the bottom is coated with a thin film of batter. When the bottom is a light brown, turn it over carefully with a wide spatula to avoid tearing it. Add your pre-chopped ingredients, then fold the sides of the crepe securely over the food. Turn the whole thing over once to brown both sides, then serve right away, with a syrup or sour cream, if desired. Alternatively, the crepes without fillings can be made ahead of time and frozen with waxed paper between them.

Many ingredients will work, as long as they're not too wet. A winning combination is always some cooked meat chopped into small pieces, grilled onions, and some cheese. For dessert, melt a little nutella or a butter/cinnamon sugar combination inside with a thinly-sliced fruit like apples, strawberries or bananas.

Somewhere along the line you may be asking yourself why you need to know so many methods and means of preparing food, particularly leftovers. That's easy: to combat boredom. It's boredom, plain and simple, both with going through the same motions in the kitchen over and over and with eating the same meal, that causes a lot of pangs to eat out. Variety really is the spice of life, and the only way to successfully overcome those expensive urges. Even "fast food" joints cost several times what you can eat more healthfully at home. Many of these meals can be made in double and triple batches, then frozen, to reheat on the days you're truly uninspired and unwilling to cook. As for the cleanup, delegate that job to someone else once in a while, then you'll have no excuse to go out.

Chapter 15
Muffin, Honey

"Quick breads," those made with chemical leavening like baking powder and baking soda, can also be modified to take extra, back-of-the-refrigerator ingredients. Getting these right is trickier than in yeast breads, in my humble opinion, because the proportions are more finicky, the recipe needs to compensate for the acid content of the mixture, and the batch is vulnerable to excessive moisture of the ingredients. This is a long way of saying I've turned out several colorful collections of hockey pucks while learning how to balance the ingredients to make snack-worthy muffins or loaves of quick breads.

There's no real skill in putting the pieces together, unlike in the yeast breads. To make, put in everything but the dry ingredients first, mix well, then add the dry stuff all at once. With quick breads, you don't want to allow the glutens to make the mix glue-like, so only mix long enough to fully incorporate the flour, and no longer. The consistency you're going for is a little thicker than pancake batter. The moisture combined with heat is what activates the leavening. Fill the greased bread pan or muffin cups only halfway to allow for expansion during baking.

Ideas for what to add to quick breads run the gamut of what yeast breads can take, which are herbs and spices, cooked grains like rice, oatmeal and tapioca, nuts, purées, and mashed or finely chopped fruits and vegetables. Finely chopped meats could also work if you're thinking of making these into a meal. As I cautioned before, determine if this batch will be sweet or savory and stay the course; the world just isn't ready for cinnamon sugar and sage muffins. Once assembled, muffins will take anywhere from 12 – 20 minutes to bake at 400F (204C).

A word about acids. Baking soda is a base. Combining it with an acid, like vinegar, results in a profusion of bubbles, as any kid with a science "volcano" kit can tell you. Those bubbles raise the batter and make light, fluffy quick breads. Acids are found in a variety of foods, like berries, buttermilk, yogurt, sour milk and sour cream. Should you use ingredients like these, you can cut the baking powder by about half and add about a half of a teaspoon baking soda per two cups of flour.

Baking powder is a combination of acid and base, which are brought together into solution with a liquid. The resultant chemical reaction speeds up by the heat of the oven, as in the case of baking soda plus acid.

Your unique quick breads will likely be with the following proportions (makes 12 muffins):

Liquid: 2/3 – 3/4 cup, depending on the moisture of other ingredients.

Eggs: 1-2. Use two if other ingredients are dense. You can whip the egg whites to stiffness and fold them into the final batter if you want lighter muffins.

Sugar: 2 tablespoons to 2/3 cup white sugar, or up to 3/4 cup brown sugar, or 1/2 cup honey or molasses.

Fat: Use 1/3 – 1/2 cup, depending on fat content of other ingredients. This ingredient can be eliminated altogether if using puréed fruits or vegetables in equal amount, though muffins will be a bit heavier and more moist.

Salt: 0 - 1 teaspoon; consider the saltiness elsewhere.

Other: Include up to 1 cup, no more than 1/2 cup cooked grains if puree is substituted for the fat.

Leavening: 1 tablespoon baking powder, or 1 1/2 teaspoon baking powder + 1/2 teaspoon baking soda. This latter option is if you have an acid in your batter.

Flour: About 2 cups, until desired consistency reached. If the batch is too dry with addition of two cups, add liquid. Sift for lighter muffins, if desired.

Here are some real-world examples of muffins I've made:

Batch #1:
> Liquid: 1/4 cup old milk plus 1/2 cup light canning syrup left over from canning apricots.
> Eggs: 2
> Sugar: 1/4 cup brown.
> Fat: I ran out of oil, but I found a 1/2 cup of apple butter that no one was eating because it looked like lake mud.
> Salt: 3/4 teaspoon.
> Other: 1/2 cup oatmeal left over from breakfast, 1/2 cup old yogurt.
> Leavening: 1 1/2 teaspoons powder, 3/4 teaspoon soda.
> Flour: 1/2 cup whole wheat, 1 1/2 cups white flour.

The result: The muffins rose just fine, making a slightly dense, moist product. The taste was sweet and mild. I suppose I could have used some cinnamon to punch up the flavor a bit, but with a spread, these passed the taste test with the munchkins.

Batch #2:
> Liquid: 1 cup of chicken broth.
> Eggs: 1.
> Sugar: None. I didn't want these muffins to be sweetened at all.
> Fat: 1/4 cup butter.
> Salt: 1 teaspoon.
> Other: 3/4 cup finely chopped leftover chicken soup ingredients[23], plus 1/2 a teaspoon of dried savory.
> Leavening: 1 tablespoon baking powder.
> Flour: 2 cups white flour.

The result: A wonderful aroma came out of the oven even before they were done. I may have overdone it on the savory, but these went well with our otherwise humble meal that night. I'm also very glad to

---

[23] This soup was a mix of chicken plus my garden harvest: cabbage, green beans, carrots, potatoes and onions

have found another way to deal with leftover soup. With the hot weather outside, no one was in the mood for another steaming bowl.

A whole batch of muffins will usually cost less than a dollar, but they can be used in a variety of ways. Every week or two, if I see enough orphaned little quantities of leftover food, I'll take the five minutes to toss a few together to make these as a quick breakfast, or some kind of snack the kids (and their friends) will inhale by mid-afternoon, or that I can serve as a side dish to add interest to what we're having for dinner. They're so portable, they're usually my first choice for a potluck contribution, too.

Versatility is the key to not wasting food, which is a key to not wasting time and money. The many ways of making quick breads can be as multi-faceted as any savings strategy comes.

Chapter 16
Four and Twenty Former
Meals Baked in a Pie

Pie, sweet or savory, comes up frequently on people's lists of the all-important Comfort Foods. There's psychologically something cheery and whole about that round shape, maybe? In any case, the first impression any pie is going to make on your crew will be positive, and there are endless combinations of what can go into that circle, including... drum roll, please.... leftovers!

No basic cookbook would dare leave out a pastry crust recipe. Moreover, the ingredients are few and what you'll always have on hand: flour, fat, salt and a liquid. Naturally the flour can have whole grains in it. The fat is best in a solid state, like butter, lard or shortening, though some people use oil and accept a less-flaky result. The liquid doesn't specifically have to be water, but most of the time it is.

Most people swear by their personal recipes for pastry crust. Fierce arguments break out during otherwise peaceful gatherings of family and friends over the best temperature, fat to use, rolling technique and so on. In the interest of peace, rather than recommend a specific recipe, this chapter will point out the universal truths of all of them. Crust tastes best if it's flaky and light. Lard and shortening are generally acknowledged to result in the flakiest crust, but butter gives the best flavor. The flakiness factor is all in the interaction of the fat with the flour, and it's very temperature-sensitive. For best results, the ingredients need to be very cold and sifting the flour isn't a bad idea, either. A top crust, if there is one for the dish, can have an egg wash to give it a nice golden color; this is just an egg yolk and about a tablespoon of milk or cream mixed well together, then brushed on before baking. Also, a top crust should be scored to allow steam to escape. Single bottom pastry shells can be pre-baked for 5-10 minutes at 450F (232C) if the ingredients are exceptionally wet, or won't be in the oven long enough to bake the crust to completion. If pre-baking, be sure to prick the bottom and sides of the shell with a fork a few times so trapped air can't warp the crust.

Certainly, the easiest pie to make is the classic pot pie. Take a soup, thicken it with cream or starch in a saucepan over low to medium heat, balance the seasonings to taste and add a pastry shell. Generally, just a crust on the top is sufficient. Bake at 400F (204C) for about 15-20 minutes until the crust is golden brown and the contents are hot and bubbly. Dinner is served.

A few recipes for pies don't require you to make a pie crust, per se, but rather they employ pancake or biscuit mixes poured into the plate to make a crust by themselves during baking. To make these, put the base food in the bottom of a greased pie plate, then make a slurry of about 3/4 of a cup of the mix, plus 2-3 eggs and 1 1/2 cups of milk. Pour this over the food and bake for about 25 minutes at 400F (204C). The result is more biscuit-like over all than a pastry-like crust. If you don't store baking mixes, you can use a scant 3/4 cup of flour, 1/2 of a teaspoon of sugar, 1/4 of a teaspoon of salt, 1/2 a teaspoon baking powder and a tablespoon of butter to substitute. If you want to store larger quantities of homemade baking mix, consult the Web for recipes that scale to larger quantities to keep the mix on hand.

Shepherd's Pie comes in many variations, and many of these resemble a basic pot pie. Instead of a pastry crust, this pie uses a topping of mashed potatoes. While pot pies tend to be more poultry-based, Shepherd's Pie usually veers in a mutton (the original, hence the name) or beef direction. Sauté at least a half of a cup of onions, brown about a pound of ground meat or use the equivalent in finely chopped or ground leftovers. Add some vegetables, also finely chopped. Very little liquid is needed for this dish; just make sure it won't completely dry out when baked. Many recipes call for lots of butter, both in the base and the topping, which helps with moisture. Load the food into the pie plate, and top with a thick layer of mashed potatoes, moistened with broth or milk to the consistency of cake frosting. The real time savings with this dish is if the mashed potatoes are made ahead from a previous meal. Cover the food completely with an even thickness of the potato, then sprinkle with paprika, if desired. Bake at 350F (177C) for about 20-25 minutes, when the meal is bubbly and the potatoes are brown on top. Gravy is optional.

Quiches are arguably a casserole, but they fit the pie description with their pastry shell, too. Because they're made with eggs as a chief component, and eggs cook quickly relative to other foods, the whole meal needs to do the same. So, once again, pre-cooked leftovers are perfect for quiche ingredients. The chief ingredients of a quiche are:

Base Food. This is the leftover that will be featured in the dish. Meats are most common, but vegetables and other ingredients are perfectly acceptable. I usually have very good results with leftover chili.

Lesser Food. This is an optional counterpart to the base food. It can be a starch such as rice or potatoes, or something to enhance the flavor, such as grated cheese, vegetables or sautéed onions. This should not be greater in quantity than the base food. A cup or so of cheese usually figures prominently in quiche recipes.

Sauce. In quiche, this is custard-based, composed of eggs plus a liquid. The liquid is usually dairy-based, but broth, vegetable or even fruit juices could also be used, as long as they're compatible with the rest of the meal.

Seasonings. To taste.

Pastry Shell. This is used only on the bottom and needs to be pre-baked to lessen absorption. Before popping it into the oven to pre-bake it, you can further seal the pastry by brushing some egg white on it. Once baked, the egg white is practically impervious to liquids. I've also seen Dijon mustard recommended as coating, too, but check compatibility with other seasonings before trying it.

The shell for quiche doesn't have to be a flour-based pastry shell. You can also make one out of leftover rice. Mix about two cups of rice with a small handful of grated cheese and an egg to hold it all together. Form it along the bottom of a greased pie plate and pre-bake for about 15 minutes at 425F (218C).

The proportions of all these ingredients per 9-inch quiche is as follows:

- Food: 2 to 3 cups.
- Sauce: To 3-4 beaten eggs, add 1 1/2 cups of any combination of milk, half–and-half, cream or other liquids, and mix well.
- Pastry: Make a single crust for a 9-inch pie.

To make the quiche: Chop the food into small pieces and season to taste. Put the food into the sealed pastry bottom and pour the custard sauce on top. Bake at 350F (177C) for 30-45 minutes, until puffy and a knife in the center comes out clean.

Finally, consider calzones or turnovers for leftover upgrades. I made a lot of these last year when the powers that be scheduled all my kid's baseball games at either lunch or dinner time, and I needed something eminently portable to take with us, lest we fall into a takeout trap on the way home. They're basically like the pies detailed before, only wrapped in the dough, so you can eat them out of hand.

To make a basic turnover, use biscuit, bread or pastry doughs. For non-dessert recipes, my personal preference is the biscuit dough. Roll out the dough to about half the regular biscuit thickness, that is about a 1/3 of an inch, then cut out circles about 3 inches in diameter. Place finely-chopped, moist-but-not-wet, seasoned food in the middle of half of the circles, leaving at good half inch on all sides. (A pre-cooked meat with a cream cheese, onion and basil combination is delicious in these!) Top each with another dough circle, then use a fork to securely crimp the edges of the two halves of dough together. Poke the top of each a couple of times with the fork, give them an egg wash if desired, then bake at about 400F (204C) for 10-12 minutes. Wrap them individually in something to keep them warm and to be able to serve them individually at the game. These freeze and reheat well, too, so you can make a lot at once, and keep the unused portion in the freezer. I even got oohs and aahs from other parents at the games over these.

I'm not sure that the term "comfort food" was originally meant to refer to the cushy savings buffer you can accumulate, but it works in the case of pies. They make saving money as easy as. . . as easy as. . .

Chapter 17
CasserOle'

I can't help it. I hear the word "casserole" and I picture a woman with cat's eyeglasses and a beehive arriving at the church potluck with a covered dish of tuna suspended in noodles and mayonnaise. There may or may not be peas in there, too, an odd bit of color in a sea of gray.

If this same image flits through your mind, too, shake it off. Casseroles aren't just for tuna, not that there's anything wrong with tuna, if you're into that sort of thing. What they *are* is a great way to make something of those odds and ends in the refrigerator. And if you liked your leftovers the first time around, you'll certainly enjoy them with a starch and sauce added; maybe even more.

So, here are the basic ingredients for concocting a casserole on the fly:

Base food. This is basically whatever you want to use up the most. Meat of some type is common; so are vegetables.

Second food. This is optional, but often enhances the flavor in some way like cheese, onions, a vegetable for color, nuts or raw celery for some crunch and so on.

A starch component. Mashed or thinly-sliced potatoes, pasta of any size and shape or rice are most commonly used. Except in the case of the thinly-sliced potatoes, the starchy ingredient should be pre-prepared. Perhaps you've noticed by now that pre-cooked starchy foods are often used in creating things out of leftovers. Often when you steam rice, mash potatoes or boil noodles, it's a good idea to make extra so you can use it to absorb the rest of the leftovers.

Sauce. The purpose of the sauce is to hold the whole thing together and to keep the mass from getting dried out. To that end, just about any thick sauce will work, most commonly white sauce, creamed soup, sour cream. During my research, nowhere did I see a specific reference to mayonnaise, so my preconceived notions of casseroles may just be flat out wrong on that score.

Topping. This is optional, but adds visual appeal, texture, and taste to the casserole. Surely no one would show her face at a church potluck without one. Ideas for toppings include buttered bread crumbs, crushed potato or corn chips, cheese, a light dusting of spices like paprika; remember those dried onion strip cracker things?

To throw a casserole together, combine up to 2 cups of chopped food that is either pre-cooked or will cook quickly, with up to 2 cups of the starch component. Add up to 2 cups of sauce. Mix all ingredients well and season to taste. Add a little liquid if the concoction seems a bit dry. Pour it all into a casserole dish (you just knew I was going to say that!), top if desired, and bake in a 350F (177C) oven for 30-45 minutes.

Bread and rice puddings are essentially casseroles, too. For about 8 servings, scald 2 cups of milk with 1/4 of a cup (half of a stick) of butter or margarine. In the meantime, mix a couple of beaten eggs with half a cup of sugar, a teaspoon of cinnamon or nutmeg or vanilla or orange peel, etc. and just a bit of salt together in a large bowl. Add 6 cups of bread cubes or 2-2 1/2 cups of

> To "scald" milk means to heat it to nearly boiling. That's just about when little bubbles form around the edges of the liquid and it starts to steam.

pre-cooked rice. You can add a half cup or so of something interesting like raisins or other dried fruit, if you've got it. Finally, add the dairy component and stir it all together. Put it in a casserole dish, and, to protect the egg from the dry heat, place the pan in about an inch of very hot water. Bake at 350F (177C) for about 40-45 minutes until a knife poked in the middle comes out clean.

Bread and rice pudding convert easily into a quick-thaw breakfast option. When making it, add an extra egg and cut the sugar to about 1/3 of a cup. Place the mix in muffin tins instead of a casserole dish, but keep the water bath. The cooking time decreases to about half.

Now you know why casseroles were so popular with housewives of yore. If she planned her leftovers correctly, any self-respecting domestic engineer could likely whip up one of these babies and have it in the oven in five minutes flat. And only one bowl got dirty to make it. These were the ultimate in fast foods before Chinese take-out. If you don't use too much dairy in the sauce, they're dirt-cheap, too. And they actually taste good, even better after being frozen[24] and reheated so the ingredients get a longer chance to blend together. As for nutritional considerations, you can quibble about all that starch, but if you use brown rice or whole-grain pasta, they're not so bad.

Look out, here comes another math problem! Let's say on an average day, all the meals take 45 minutes to prepare. By this, I mean 45 minutes of your active involvement, i.e. chopping, pouring, adding something to the mixer, etc. If that still seems low, remember that bulk-cooking often yields three to five meals for a half hour of steady chopping and some meals like oatmeal, soups and casseroles take less than ten minutes of hands-on time to assemble.

Very conservatively speaking, the savings from home-cooked meals versus convenience food is, say, $10 a day, assuming $3 per meal and a buck on snacks. Remember that the savings is much higher over fast food or restaurants, but convenience foods are the closest competition to homemade. That $10 of saved consumption dollars is actually worth more in earned dollars. Think about it; to get a job and acquire that ten spot, you'd have to get a wage high enough to pay all the taxes and taken out of it, usually over twenty percent. You'd therefore need to earn about $13 to be able to take home $10.

So, saving $10 for 45 minutes of work is the equivalent of about $13 for the same amount of time earned in a job. What's the hourly wage for this pursuit, then? $13 earned in the span of three-quarters of an hour works out to an hourly wage of $17.33. That's pretty respectable middle-class remuneration, don't you think? "Moonlighting" by making scratch meals at home instead of buying

---

[24] Don't freeze potato casseroles; these will get somewhat rubbery.

convenience foods at the supermarket will net you the equivalent of earning $4745 at an outside job, no commute (or pantyhose!) required. This hourly wage goes even higher if your family is currently in the habit of eating take-out or fast food all the time, or, gulp, sit-down restaurant meals.

You don't have to sweat the interview, and you can eat the food. This is the easiest second job you'll ever get.

Chapter 18
Feats of Dairy Do

In my valiant struggle to feed the family nutritiously and still have enough money left over to clothe and shelter them, too, I find myself nearly undone by the problem of dairy. A lot of fruits and vegetables I can grow. Meat I can substitute among various kinds of animal sources, depending upon what's cheapest, and further stretch it by making it more of a flavoring than the main meal, and still get adequate protein. I even bought an electric mill so I can store large amounts of different whole grains whenever I find them cheap, and then make the flour myself when I need it, so it can't go rancid. Similarly, I can stock up on great sales of imperishable foods. However, so many of my strategies come to a screeching halt at the threshold of the dairy conundrum. Milk products are mostly perishable, so I can't store them on a shelf. Most don't even freeze well or they take up a huge amount of space, so I can't stock up and store a lot when they're cheap. There aren't a lot of substitutes available. And, I can't keep my own cow in the backyard. Or even a nanny goat, for that matter.

I guess the best answer would be to walk away from this expensive food and find our calcium, protein and flavoring-fat elsewhere, but our family very much enjoys milk, yogurt, sour cream, cream, butter and cheese, so we'd feel pinched in their absence or scarcity. But do these limitations mean I'm going to meekly hand over my wallet to Bossy from Jersey? NooOOOoo! This is yet another challenge. Exploring every possible angle of the problem just might yield some solutions to bring down the cost of dairy products.

First, I recommend that your family convert to non-fat milk, if possible. Generally, the more fat, the more expensive the milk. And who needs the fat? Say you go through two gallons a week, and save fifty cents per gallon by making the switch. The difference over the course of a year is over $100 and several pounds' worth of calories. To make the change, slowly mix in a higher ratio of nonfat milk to what you regularly drink until you gradually get used to the new consistency. Once you're accustomed to nonfat, you'll never look back.

Second, take a long look at powdered dairy products, which may not be ideal in all applications, but work fine for most cooking and baking. The ability to store anything long term lends itself to savings because you can "buy low, use high," and you can buy in bulk, saving you time and gasoline on what would be multiple trips to obtain it fresh. Dairy prices fluctuate quite a bit depending upon market forces, so if milk prices were a lot cheaper a year or so ago, then powdered milk will now reflect last year's price somewhat.

As far as non-perishable dairy options go, I am aware that there is ultra-pasteurized, boxed milk that can store on shelves, too, but I dislike it for two big reasons. One, storing it wet takes up much more space than dry, and who among us has unlimited space? Two, it's absolutely awful. That burnt aftertaste can't even be disguised in muffins or sauces. Thankfully, it's also more expensive than fresh or powdered, so unless I have some compelling reason, like a gun to my head, I'll give it a miss.

Speaking of powdered dairy products, even fat can be freeze-dried now! There are powdered versions of milk, buttermilk, sour cream, cream, butter, cheeses and yogurt these days. I've been all over the Web researching the cheapest sources I can find for these products, but so far only the powdered milk is a really good deal. Regular fresh milk is around $3.30/gallon; I was able to buy powdered for $1.58/gallon reconstituted.[25] However, the cheapest price I could find for butter was almost eight bucks a pound

---

[25] I found a good deal on whole dried milk from the Honeyville Food Company, honeyvillegrain.com.

reconstituted weight, and I'd have to buy a 50-pound sack. Since butter's running somewhere south of three bucks a pound last I looked, I'll pass for now. It's sheer speculation on my part, but I'm guessing that the technology to dehydrate fats is still somewhat new and complicated, so not a lot of companies are doing it, yet. I suggest we all keep tabs on these products, and may be pleasantly surprised some day. One final note: when you do search the Web, be leery of sites devoted to emergency preparedness or backpacking. Most of them are charging rip-off prices. Go to the home storage supply sites.

Of course, when butter is reasonably cheap, I'll buy as much as I can fit into the freezer, but capacity is very limited. I was thrilled to find out that butter can be canned, and then stored at room temperature for years. Dozens of websites detail the procedure, but the gist of it is to bring the butter to a slow boil, let it simmer for a while, then pour into hot, sterilized jars and seal. Once the lids are vacuum-sealed, to keep the butter from separating, it's important to shake it occasionally while it is cooling back down to room temperature. After that, it can be stored just like your jams.

There is still something more I can do about the price of dairy. I can make my own dairy products from plain milk and, in some cases, this is significantly cheaper

> Check out http://www.endtimesreport.com/canning_butter.html for some complete instructions on preserving butter.

than if I buy the processed product at the store. It is possible to make your own butter, yogurt, ice cream, sour cream, cottage cheese, cheese, buttermilk and whipped cream. A few quick calculations will tell you if it's worth the effort.

In the case of making **yogurt,** I've run the numbers and I can save money. This is because I can make it based on my cheap, powdered milk. When all is said and done, my yogurt works out to about a third of the cost of the cheapest store-bought stuff. It's very easy to make, too. You need the proper bacteria to start, so make an initial trip to the store to buy fresh plain yogurt with active cultures. I hate to admit it, but most of the time the cheap stuff is "dead on arrival," so splurge to make sure you get live culture; you won't have to buy it again, unless your freezer fails.

Once you get home, put your culture on the counter and let it warm to room temperature. In the meantime, pour 7 cups of water into the top part of a double boiler. Add about 3 3/4 cups powdered milk. This amount of powdered milk makes the milk, and ultimately the yogurt, thicker. Cover, and heat the constituted milk in the double boiler until it reaches 185F (85C). This kills off some bacteria that would compete with your culture. When the milk reaches the desired temperature, which only takes a few minutes, cool it down to 131F (55C). You can stick it in the refrigerator if you want; my preference is to put the pan in a larger pan with ice water in it, and stir, which takes less than five minutes. I'm not known for my patience. Once the milk is cool enough, pour a little into a cup and add at least a couple of tablespoons of culture; more doesn't hurt at all. Stir to break up the yogurt, when smooth, dump the whole thing into the rest of the milk and stir to evenly distribute the culture. Pour some milk into a small cup to make your future starting culture, and pour the rest into two clean quart jars. Seal the lids.

Now all the yogurt-in-training needs are warmth and time. Some people just wrap up the jars tightly in a rag and put it somewhere draft-free. Others warm theirs slightly in an oven with the light on. Yogurt bacteria start to die at temperatures above 131F (55C), but they won't do much below 104F (40C), so try to stay in the high side of that range. I like to pour the water left over from the double boiler into a small cooler and add water from the cooling pan until the temperature is 131F (55C). There's my warming chamber. Leave it alone for at least three hours, then check if it's ready. If not, make sure it's still warm enough and wait another three hours. You'll hopefully have yogurt by then. If not, your expensive starter yogurt didn't have live cultures after all. Once the yogurt has set up, put the small cup of yogurt in the freezer for starting the next batch. Just thaw to room temperature to use. Enjoy the rest in smoothies, flavored with fruit or jam, flavored with Indian or Greek spices, in baking, on potatoes, whatever you like to do with it.

Comparing homemade ice cream with the cheapest store-bought version yields little or no savings from the effort, but of course the taste is exceptional, so make it for party contributions. Whipping your own cream is cheaper than buying the stuff from the can, and you can control the sweetness. Recipes and instructions for making **ice cream** and **whipping cream** are available in most basic cookbooks, or in the instructions that come with ice cream makers. Of course, if you whip the cream too vigorously, past the point of hard whipped peaks, you'll make **butter**. Add a little salt to keep butter fresh longer.

You can make your own **buttermilk**, sort of. In days of yore, buttermilk was what separated out of cream that was agitated enough to form into butter. Now the "buttermilk" sold in stores is basically another form of yogurt: same milk, different culture. Therefore, you can make this kind of buttermilk in the exact same way you can make yogurt, only use a buttermilk with active cultures as the starter. The good news from a cost-savings standpoint is that the starting milk can be constituted from milk powder. Use about a half of a cup of "live" buttermilk per three cups of milk. Leave undisturbed at room temperature until thickened. Don't forget to save a cup or so to put into the freezer to make your next batch.

Sour cream and **cream cheese** are both made by inoculating cream or cream and milk with buttermilk. In both cases, you warm the cream just to room temperature and add buttermilk of the same temperature. That, plus the time for the culture to multiply and sour the cream is all that sour cream requires. With cream cheese, you also need to add rennet, which curdles the milk. After a few hours, you can drain off the whey from the milk solids, and you have a simple cheese. Don't toss the whey! It's very nutritious, so use it in your next bread batch. So far, in my local market, neither of these products is much different in price than the milk needed to make them.

Cottage cheese is another easy modification to milk and likely to be worth learning how to make, especially since you can use powdered nonfat milk as the basis for it. One gallon of

I found precise instructions for making cream cheese at: http://biology.clc.uc.edu/Fankhaus er/cheese/Cream_Cheese.htm

nonfat milk makes about a pound of cottage cheese. There are a few different ways to make cottage cheese. One method of making cottage cheese is to start off with firm yogurt and then heat it at 115F (46C) for about 25 minutes until the curds are firm to the touch, after which you strain out the whey, wash the curds in cold water and lightly salt the curds that remain.

A second method of making cottage cheese is to start with firm buttermilk. Cut the curd with a knife into uniform 3/4 inch cubes, then pour hot water (120F or 49C) over them to a depth of an inch. Heat them very slowly only rising about three degrees F (two degrees C) every 10 minutes or so, while rotating the curds every few minutes gently so as not to break them up. After an hour and fifteen minutes, the curds should be well separated from the whey. Drain the curds and wash them with water, first lukewarm, then very cold. Salt lightly and mix gently. If you want firmer cottage cheese, hang it somewhere in cheesecloth and let it drain more.

Still a third method for making cottage cheese involves adding either rennet by itself or rennet in combination with buttermilk to make the curds. The cooking and draining procedures are the same.

Finally, adding rennet to milk with a specific culture is also the basis of **hard cheese**. Cheese is like bread; the regional cultures determine the regional cheeses, and no two are exactly alike. Making your own cheese may be fun for the sake of a hobby, but in my research I've found the cost savings over the cost of buying the milk is minimal for the work involved.

Dairy, dairy quite contrary; how do my dollars grow? When confronting the high cost of any food, ask yourself the following questions:

1. Can I just do without this particular food?
2. Is there an acceptable lower-cost substitute, at least temporarily?
3. Can I cut down my usage of this product?
4. Have I thoroughly researched all possible sources to find the cheapest one?
5. Can it be made shelf stable so I can buy it in bulk or stock up on a good sale?
6. Can I enter into a cooperative buying arrangement with others to take advantage of bulk or wholesale savings, even if the item is perishable?
7. Can I make this product myself for sufficiently less money that it's worth the expense of my time?

Very rarely will the answer be "no" on all counts. There's almost always some angle you can exploit to bring down your expenditures in each food category. Most of the work in saving money is mental.

Chapter 19
Top Ten Uses for Dead Bread

I'm sure in the highly secretive world of convenience food production, no one can answer this question for me without subsequently having to kill me, but I wish I knew exactly what it is about store bought bread that lets it sit on the counter for a week without getting hard and/or moldy. Is it the partially hydrogenated soybean oil? The sodium stearoyl lactylate, maybe? Those yummy monoglycerides that have the kids clamoring for more?

When I make a two-loaf batch of my bread, I can usually count on the family wolfing down the first loaf within a couple of hours. Breakfast or lunch the next day takes up most of the rest, but there's always that last quarter of a loaf that by Day Three closely resembles a loofah sponge. So here's a new challenge: What to Do with Old Bread. Naturally, when a gauntlet like that is thrown, we can't just give up and feed the old loaf to the birds. Below are some of my personal favorite ways to avoid wasting the Staff of Life.

10. Bread crumbs. Simply take dried-out bread of any type, break it into pieces into the blender, cover the top and turn it on until the crumbs are of the desired consistency. Use to top casseroles, bread fish and chicken, in meatloaf; you can even make cookies out of them! Search for "bread crumb cookie recipe" on the Internet; you'll find dozens of variations. So long as they're kept dry in a sealed container, bread crumbs will also store at room temperature for a couple of weeks. They'll keep in the freezer indefinitely.

9. Bread cubes. This works best with French, sourdough or rye breads. Cut the bread into cubes. Dry the cubes by tossing them into a still-warm oven after baking, stirring once in a while. These are good for poultry stuffing and croutons. Bread cubes have the same storage requirements as bread crumbs.

8. Croutons. Take your bread cubes and drizzle them with a little oil, then sprinkle lightly with salt, and spices like dried oregano and sage. Bake for about ten minutes at 300F (149C), or put them in for about twenty minutes just as you've turned off the oven from making bread. These taste wonderful in soups and salads. Don't store them at room temperature for more than a week because of the oil in them, which could go rancid.

7. French Toast. Beat eggs and add milk up to half the volume of the eggs. Add some cinnamon sugar and mix well. Slice your old bread, and soak the slices in the egg mixture. Fry these on a lightly-greased medium-high griddle like pancakes, turning once until golden brown on both sides. Serve hot with pancake syrup, butter or jam. French Toast also freezes well.

6. Welsh Rarebit. Take an old, dried-out slice of bread. Pour a cheesy white sauce over it. Yell, "Dinner!" and serve.

5. Science Experiments. Let a piece of bread get really, really moldy. The yellow juice that you can squeeze out of the blue-green mold is unrefined penicillium chrysogenum, better known as, simply, penicillin. No, I wouldn't actually try to use it, but this is your science lesson for today. Besides, I can't think of any other possible use for old bread, other than your compost pile, once mold enters the picture. It's even bad for the birds at that point.

4. Charlotte. Alternate buttered stale, thinly-sliced bread or crumbs with sweetened, cooked fruit (like for a cobbler). Top with the bread, sprinkle with sugar, and bake at 375F (191C) for about half an hour. This makes a cobbler-like dessert.

3. Desiccant. Thoroughly dry a hunk or slice of bread, then store it with your brown sugar. It will wick up the moisture in the air and keep the sugar from clumping. Replace as needed.

2. Oven Cheese Fondue. To serve five: Beat five eggs well. Add a teaspoon of salt, a dash of pepper and 2 to 3 cups of grated cheese, and mix. Now add 2 1/2 cups of hot milk with 4 cups cubed bread.

Pour it all into a greased 7 X 11 inch baking pan, and bake at 325F (163C) for half an hour until set. This recipe comes from the *More-with-Less Cookbook,* by Doris Janzen Longacre. This is a terrific compendium of recipes mostly made from basic staples that I almost always have around the house, and the meals turn out great. I think it's out of print, but used copies are still floating around the Webosphere.

And the Number One use for dead bread is...

1. Bruschetta! This works with any bread, but I think sourdough tastes best: Brush an old, dried-up, thin slice of bread with oil, tomato paste or pesto. Top with cheese, basil, onions, peppers, pepperoni or any other way you'd fix a pizza, then broil for a couple of minutes to melt it all together. Serve. Yum!

None of us like to admit it, but we've all had those moments of crushing disappointment when we open the bread box and find nothing but fresh, soft, moist bread. Buck up, promise yourself you'll plan better next time, close the box and wait. Your patience will be rewarded in a day or two with wonderful dried-out, hard, stale foundations for many delicious meal options.[26]

---

[26] Isn't "Dry County," by the B52's about this? I think the words go something like, "When the blues kick you in the head; 'Cuz you're outta dead bread that you wa-anted...." Remember their advice: "Just sit on the porch and swing."

Conclusion
Putting It All Together

This book has certainly detailed the math and mechanics of how to save money on food, and why most of us should work harder at controlling this area of spending, but how does this look in a scenario close to the real world? Can one really save so much money on food without slaving away in the kitchen or grocery store for hours a day?

To answer that question, let's look at an evening in the life of two hypothetical families: The Frugalle's and the BrokeMeisters. The Frugalle's have committed themselves over the years to saving as much money as possible in the area of their food spending, and they're pretty good at it. The BrokeMeisters have been sucked into every myth about what a typical middle-class family is supposed to buy, as defined by our culture and advertising agencies. They spend to the bleeding edge of their paychecks every month . . . and they're pretty good at it.

Sunday evening after the kids have gone to bed, we find Mrs. Frugalle in front of her white board, planning the week's meals. There's a Scout activity on Monday night, Mrs. Frugalle has to work late on Tuesday night, Mr. Frugalle will be home late on Thursday night, and no one in the family is allowed to forget the Big Game Friday evening, as Junior has mentioned it every waking moment for days already.

Mrs. Frugalle pulls a whole chicken out of the freezer and sets it on the counter. Monday, she'll cut it up and oven-fry it, since she'll be home early enough to get the chicken in the oven an hour before it has to be ready in time for Junior's Night Hike. She'll serve that meal with some boiled potatoes, vegetables and a salad. When she cuts up the chicken, she'll toss the back, giblets, vegetable peelings, celery leaves and a cut-up onion into her slow cooker, and let them simmer in water all night. Total preparation time for Monday night's whole meal, plus tomorrow's salad, plus the broth is about half an hour.

Looking at her options for Tuesday's dinner, she knows she'll likely have leftover potatoes, fried chicken, chicken pieces from the broth and a good soup stock, so she mentally plans a potato soup to use up the potatoes and some of the stock, to be made in about 15 minutes in the morning, and ready to reheat when the family gets home that night to eat without her. The fried chicken will go in lunches.

For Wednesday, since the family will all be home, she'll spend about half an hour of her time to make batches of muffins and bread, using some of the sourdough batter for Pizza Night. This is always a hit with the clan, and a good way to use up some garden produce. Leftover pizza makes fabulous lunches, too.

Mr. Frugalle did the grocery shopping this week, and spied a clearance basket full of unlabeled cans for pennies each. Knowing his wife's ingenuity, he bought about twenty cans to surprise her. They had a good laugh about this. She won't open anything, yet, but on Tuesday or Wednesday, she'll pick something and plan Thursday's meal around it, whatever it is. On her whiteboard, she writes down, "Mystery Night." She'll make sure it reheats well to accommodate her husband's late night.

For Friday, Mrs. Frugalle knows there will be enough chicken scraps and potato soup left over to get a good start on a casserole, which is good, because she'll be beat and she needs something that won't spill to take to the game. On Friday evening, Mr. Frugalle casually mentions that his company is merging with another, which might lay off his department. Mrs. Frugalle looks worried.

Mr. Frugalle, ever sensitive to his wife's concerns, asks what's wrong.

"Well," she replies, "if you do get the time off, I have a honey-do list a mile long. Don't start a new job right away." They exchange more laughter.

All this Sunday planning took about ten minutes. Now Mrs. Frugalle just needs to pack the family's lunches with the bread she made over the weekend, and check what's available for breakfast in the morning. She decides she'll make oatmeal, since what's left over can go into Wednesday's muffins. She measures the water in the pan and the oats next to it on the counter, so she won't have to think much in the morning. Another ten minutes has elapsed, and she plops in front of the television, done for the day.

Next door to the Frugalle's live the Brokemeisters. No one thought through the week ahead, each day comes crashing down on them like a car speeding towards a couple of dazzled deer. When Mr. Brokemeister went to the grocery store, he bought several boxes of his favorite brand of cereal and some frozen dinners that looked good. He came across a new breakfast bar that promised "whole grain goodness," so he got some for the kids, to eat on their way out the door every morning. At the supermarket, Mr. Brokemeister waved politely to that nut Mr. Frugalle who was pushing a cart full of clearance stuff that had no rhyme or reason, reflecting that there's one in every neighborhood.

On Monday, their kid had to be at a Scout function that night, so they had some of the frozen dinners since "who can cook on a weeknight?" On Tuesday, Mrs. Brokemeister had to work late, so Mr. Brokemeister took the kids out to fast food. On Wednesday, Mrs. Brokemeister suggested they all go out to a nice family restaurant, since "everyone's home tonight." On Thursday, Mrs. Brokemeister heated up some more frozen dinners. On Friday, they bought hotdogs and sodas at the Big Game. School lunches are three dollars a day for each of the kids; the Brokemeisters reason that it's a good deal, since it's cheaper than fast food, and certainly not worth their time to make lunches every day. Much of the bread and fresh produce that they buy every week goes bad

Visit http://www.simpletonsolutions.com for helpful links, tips and tricks, and reader feedback!

and gets tossed. By sheer coincidence, Mr. Brokemeister announced on Friday night that he hoped to pick up an overtime shift all day Saturday, as they're "going to be a little short this month."

Food is more expensive than we realize, because through the sheer "morning, noon and night" repetition, the steady drip of extra money spent accumulates quickly. Ninety percent of the effort needed to slow down the leak only takes one percent more time, and that is to plan. Plan your meals around what you have, starting with the most perishable foods and then from your storage. Once the plan is in place, execution invariably takes less time than the extra trips to the grocery store to get convenience foods, the evenings spent in restaurants, the take-out runs and certainly less time than the extra hours at work to pay for all the overpriced meals.

There's also a certain sense of empowerment in using one's strategic intellect to tackle the problem of maximum nutrition for the lowest possible price and effort. It's a truly engaging pursuit, certainly lucrative, but more than that; it builds a sense of community and it's emotionally satisfying. We frugally-minded foodies love to swap stories about our many "victories" and to help each other, and we keep up our skinflint practices long after the financial crisis that initially brought us to this practice is over, because it's entertaining, like solving puzzles and logic problems.

So get out there and rack up some good success stories, then email them to me: elise@simpletonsolutions.com. I'll post my favorites on the website so we can all celebrate!

Appendix A

**Weight to Volume Conversions
Of Common Dry Baking Ingredients[27]**

One Pound of:	Equals	Cups
Flour, Bread		3.57
Flour, Cake		3.31
Flour, Cake, sifted		4.71
Flour, White, All-Purpose		3.64
Flour, White, All-Purpose, sifted		3.90
Flour, Whole Wheat		3.78
Oats, Rolled		5.04
Rice, Brown, Short		2.39
Rice, Brown, Long		2.45
Rice, White, Short		2.27

---

[27] Weight for specific volumes depends somewhat on moisture content, compaction and the like, but these are good approximate figures for calculating how much you're spending in recipes. Just don't bet your life on these being perfectly precise.

Rice, White, Long 2.45

Sugar, Brown, firmly packed 2.27

Sugar, Powdered 3.25

Sugar, Powdered, sifted 4.00

Sugar, White 2.25

One Ounce of:	**Equals**	**Teaspoons**
Baking Powder		6.25
Baking Soda		7.14
Chili Powder		10.9
Cinnamon		12.3
Cocoa Powder		9.0
Corn Starch		10.62
Cream of Tartar		9.0
Paprika		13.5
Pumpkin Pie Spice		16.7
Salt		5.0
Yeast, Active Dry		9.0

Appendix B

Equivalent Measures

3 Teaspoons	=	1 Tablespoon
4 Tablespoons	=	¼ Cup
5 1/3 Tablespoons	=	1/3 Cup
16 Tablespoons	=	1 Cup
2 Cups	=	1 Pint
2 Pints (4 Cups)	=	1 Quart
4 Quarts (16 Cups)	=	1 Gallon

Appendix C

Highly Recommended Reading

Ball Blue Book, The Guide to Home Canning and Freezing, © 1994 by Alltrista Corporation, Muncie, Indiana 47303-0729

The Complete Tightwad Gazette, by Amy Dacyczyn, © by Villard Books, a division of Random House, Inc., New York, New York

The Encyclopedia of Country Living, by Carla Emery, © 2003 by Carla Emery

The Essential Cook, Everything You Really Need to Know about Foods and Cooking, by Charles Delmar, © 1989 by Hill House Publishing Company, Chapel Hill, North Carolina

More-with-Less Cookbook, by Doris Janzen Longacre, © 1977 by Herald Press, Scottdale, PA 15683

Index

T

tempura, 71
therm, 25

U

USDA Plant Hardiness Zone
  Map, 19

V

vitamins, 10

W

Welsh Rarebit, 94
whipped cream, 90

Y

yeast, 58

Printed in the United States
130905LV00001B/1-249/P